D0948942

From Couch to Conditioned:
A Beginner's Guide to Getting Fit

Tai Chi for Beginners

CONOR KILGALLON AND ANDREW AUSTIN

New York

This edition published in 2012 by:

The Rosen Publishing Group, Inc.
29 East 21st Street
New York, NY 10010

Library of Congress
Cataloging-in-Publication Data

Kilgallon, Conor.
Tai chi for beginners / Conor Kilgallon, Andrew Austin.
p. cm.—(From couch to conditioned: A beginner's guide to getting fit)
Includes bibliographical references and index.
ISBN 978-1-4488-4816-4 (library binding)
ISBN 978-1-4488-4820-1 (pbk.)
ISBN 978-1-4488-4824-9 (6-pack)
1. Tai chi. I. Austin, Andrew. II. Title.
GV504.K53 2012
613.7'148—dc22

2011008280

Manufactured in the United States of America

CPSIA Compliance Information: Batch #S11YA: For further information, contact Rosen Publishing, New York, New York, at 1-800-237-9932.

contents

the forms 30

the learning program 84

introduction

In the early morning mist in a clearing beneath the trees, an old man flows effortlessly through a series of gentle movements. The trickle of a nearby stream calms his spirit as he bends and turns like the branches of a tree flexing in the wind. Old and wise, he glides like a crane floating in the sky. He is at one with the world. Such tranquil images are often associated with the practice of tai chi—and with good reason. Somehow these simple movements provide a private, inner sanctuary from the rigors of modern daily life. Chan Buddhists believe that truth and enlightenment are found within, asking the eternal question—if you cannot find the truth right where you are, where else do you expect to find it?

The emphasis of our modern world can make us feel that to develop as individuals and satisfy our personal needs we should travel to exotic places, listen to soothing music, burn the right scents and candles, and involve ourselves in other such external activities. These things may help us, but we should not forget that the deepest enrichment is found within. Tai chi aims to teach us this. Through the slow, meditative movements of the tai chi form, it is possible to uncover aspects of ourselves that would otherwise remain undiscovered.

patient learning

This book is intended as a guide to those wishing to learn a little about tai chi. Remember, however, that the guidance offered in any text is no substitute for a qualified and experienced teacher. As with any art, tai chi can look simple when it is performed well. However, it will take time, practice, and patience to reach a good level. Improvements will be gradual, but well worth the effort.

Put simply, tai chi advocates the use of gentle exercise and controlled breathing, so if you can move and breathe, you can learn tai chi. The prerequisite for learning this extraordinary art is patience. By learning slowly and surely, you will reveal many benefits from tai chi practice. It is like walking—go too fast, and you will arrive exhausted and tired. At a gentle pace, however, you have time to take in your surroundings,

ANCIENT ART IN ANY LANGUAGE

The ancient art of tai chi has been written about in countless forms—from the oldest scripts passed down through generations to magazines offering the latest fashions for achieving good health. It has been written about, talked about, dissected, and analyzed in almost every language.

Until the romanization of the Chinese language (called Pinyin), the term "tai chi" has been spelled in many different ways, such as "tai chi," "t'ai chi," "taiji," "tai chi chuan," "t'ai chi ch'uan," and "taijiquan," all referring to the same discipline. The correct Pinyin spelling is "taijiquan," although the "tai chi" spelling is the most popular and will be used here.

enjoy the views, breathe, and arrive relaxed, refreshed, and invigorated.

If you have any doubts as to whether tai chi can suit your needs, consult your doctor. Keep in mind that the postures should be practiced gently and without strain to prevent any unwelcome discomfort.

try before you decide

It is often said that you should learn only from the most knowledgeable source to reach the highest goals. It is also said that a good teacher may not necessarily perform well and equally that a great performer may not teach effectively. Perhaps then it is wiser to find a teacher with whom you feel comfortable, someone you can understand clearly. It can be helpful to determine how well a teacher conveys his teaching by watching other students in the class. A student of several years should look more competent than one of a few months, but then learning ability does vary from person to person, so talk to the other students to get their individual perspectives.

A new student to tai chi should attend several classes before deciding whether or not it is the right one. The first lesson will be simple and often repetitive, so you shouldn't judge an entire discipline on the strength of a single lesson. After all, can anyone play the guitar competently after just one hour of instruction? A class should always be experienced for a month or so to provide a clear indication of how things run.

FINDING A GOOD TEACHER

Many types of tai chi classes are available. Some classes teach postures and correct body alignment. Some teach the martial applications hidden within the forms. Others concentrate on focusing energy on a particular part of the body and then guiding it to another. These are all different aspects of tai chi, which come together to form a whole. Here we are concerned primarily with the physical aspects of the art.

Because the tai chi path is one of constant learning and refinement, you can never truly claim to have learned all there is to know about the subject. This means that knowledge varies from one teacher to the next. In the search for a suitable teacher, first identify three basic requirements:

1

Do you like the teacher?

Can the teacher convey the various ideas clearly and effectively? Do your personalities clash? It is of no use learning from a great master for whom you have no respect.

2

Is the teacher knowledgeable?

Who did the teacher learn from? Has the teacher practiced tai chi for a long time? It would be unreasonable to learn such an intricate discipline from someone who has been learning for only a year.

3

Does the style suit your needs?

Do you like the style of tai chi being taught? Does it suit your needs? For example, if you suffer from joint problems, a style with very low stances and difficult postures will not benefit you.

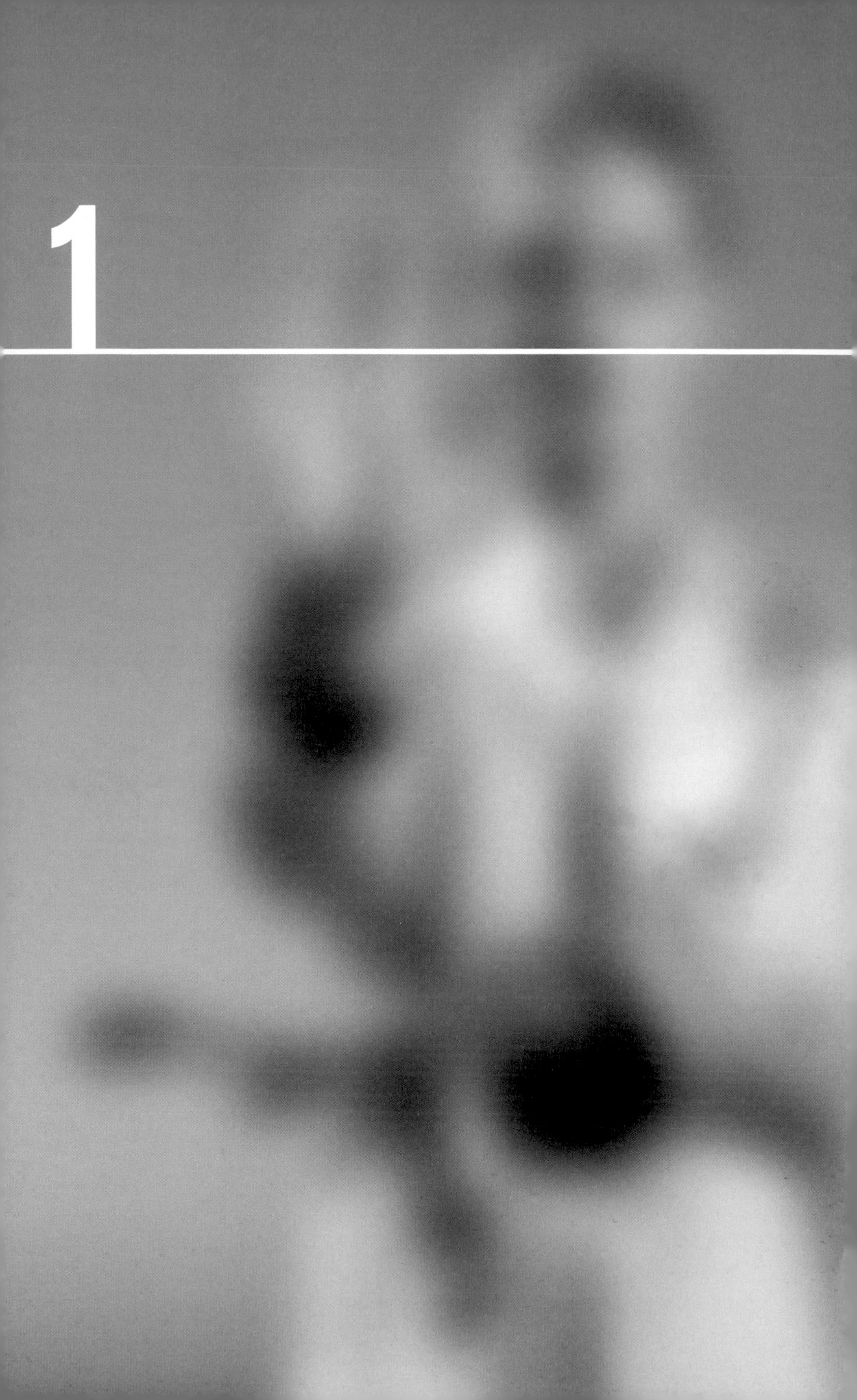
1

origins of tai chi

Tai chi is an ancient practice, but it does not exist in just one form. This chapter explores the origins of tai chi and its different styles, and tells you how you can improvc your health by regulating your body, your breath, and your mind, and by learning how to relax.

what is tai chi?

The Chinese term "tai chi" has many meanings. The Pinyin, or Mandarin Chinese system of spelling according to sounds, writes the expression as "taijiquan," which breaks down into "supreme" (tai), "ultimate" (ji), and "fist" (quan). The common use of "quan" implies a boxing method or sequence, so "taijiquan" is sometimes referred to as "soft boxing." Tai chi represents a superior system of human development and contributes positively to all aspects of the human being. To fully appreciate the technique, you need to allow yourself to be immersed fully in its movements. The body should relax and coordinate, the breath should be controlled and deepened, and the mind should be still and calm.

The mystical art of tai chi originates from the fighting arts of China. Although many argue that tai chi is the oldest form of methodical fighting technique, this is unlikely. The oldest forms of fighting, which can be traced back to the early sixth century, would have been much simpler and would have required less skill in their application. It is more likely that tai chi is the result of the development of many other disciplines, such as calisthenics and ancient breath-control techniques, as well as evolving medical knowledge.

Tai chi retains its effectiveness as a devastating martial art as well as a powerful means to improve health by reducing stress and anxiety. The postures are practiced in a slow, deliberate way, using the mind to guide the body.

the history of tai chi

Because most of the population in ancient China was illiterate, the origins of tai chi were never accurately documented. Although some attempts were made to record the theory and practice of the technique permanently, the primitive and costly printing methods made such documentation impractical. So an understanding of tai chi was handed down from one generation to the next through oral communication and active demonstration. In this way the teachings of tai chi evolved with each passing generation. Even today, two students of the same teacher will perform the same movements with subtle differences.

The famous Chinese doctor Hua Tuo, who lived toward the end of the Han Dynasty in the third century A.D., believed that both physical and mental exercises were paramount to the development of good health. He thought that nature held the key to developing human potential and well-being and that human exercise should imitate the movements and inner nature of animals. Hua Tuo systemized an exercise method based on the movements of animals and birds known as the "Five Animal Games," which aided digestion and circulation. His theory is still widely practiced today in many martial arts. The names of some of the tai chi postures used today show the technique's strong links with nature and animals and therefore with this philosophy, with examples such as "parting the wild horse's mane," "white crane spreads its wings," "repulse the monkey," "grasp the peacock's tail," "box tiger's ears," and "snake creeps down."

Although no one is certain, it is thought that the technique of tai chi was first conceived in either the twelfth or the fifteenth century (depending on the source) by Zhang Sanfeng of the Wudang Mountains in the Hupen Province of China. He is believed to have developed combat techniques that were designed to increase the flow of "chi," or energy, through the body. The roots of tai chi as we know it today were first introduced by Chen Wangding in the Henan Province in the early years of the Qing Dynasty in the seventeenth century. This technique of "soft boxing" was in fact quite violent, intended to inflict harm on the opponent with the "softness" based around the idea of absorbing the opponent's aggressive energy and turning it back against him.

In the late eighteenth century, the highly skilled martial artist Wang Zongyue wrote a book that introduced the term "tai chi" or "taijiquan." In this period, tai chi had many fast and explosive movements and it was only much later, as the need for aggressive combat lessened, that nonviolent tai chi came into its own. Yang Luchan in the nineteenth century modified the original "Chen" style and took the new exercise to Beijing. His translation of it into a gentle, more graceful art won it many admirers and made it accessible to all. The technique has continued to evolve, and in the early twentieth century Yang Chengfu, grandson of Yang Luchan, promoted and organized the "Yang" style that is close to its current practiced form.

THE BEIJING YANG

The original "forms" of tai chi—meaning the individual sequences of movements that flow from one to the next in a specific order and with a clear beginning and end—contained a great number of movements and would have taken considerable practice to master. Once complete, a single sequence could last as long as 30 minutes or more. This prompted the introduction of a shorter, simpler form.

The martial arts division of the National Physical Education Committee in China in 1956 devised the 24-step simplified "Beijing Yang" form that was promoted by the Chinese government. These 24 postures were based on 20 of the 34 postures that Yang Chengfu developed and contained the essence of the "Yang" principles.

This, and other modified forms of the original technique, now have a worldwide following and are associated with many health benefits, including the ability to calm the mind, relax the body, relieve stress, give greater strength, fend off illness, and aid recovery.

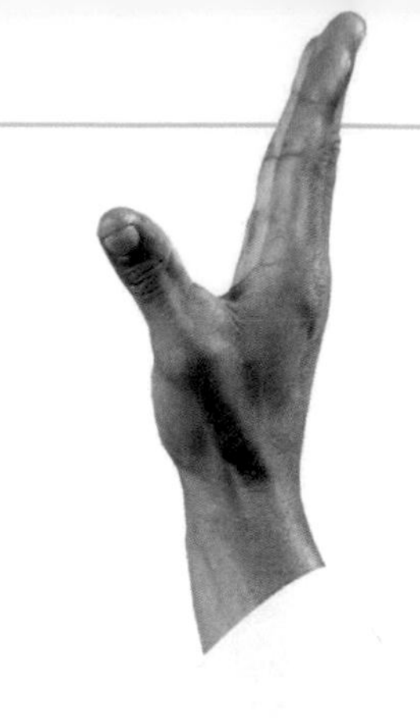

tai chi styles

There are five main styles of tai chi: Chen, Yang, Wu, Hao, and Sun. These are all family names and therefore family styles. The Chen style is arguably the most obvious in its martial application, as fighting techniques can be clearly recognized within its forms. Considered the oldest of the internal martial arts, the movements of the Chen style express fast and explosive techniques, as well as some slower, gentler moves.

The Yang style was born from the Chen style (the two villages being in close proximity to one another). This style is much more subtle in its approach and has no obvious explosive movements. The Yang style is generally performed more slowly and in higher stances, which makes it easier and more accessible than the other styles. The Yang style is referred to as the "large frame" method and is characterized by large, flowing movements that gently stretch the limbs with open, bold gestures. The transition from one posture to the next is seamless and is performed at a slow, even tempo.

The remaining three styles of Wu, Hao, and Sun adopt different approaches to the art of fighting, although they share common principles within their structure.

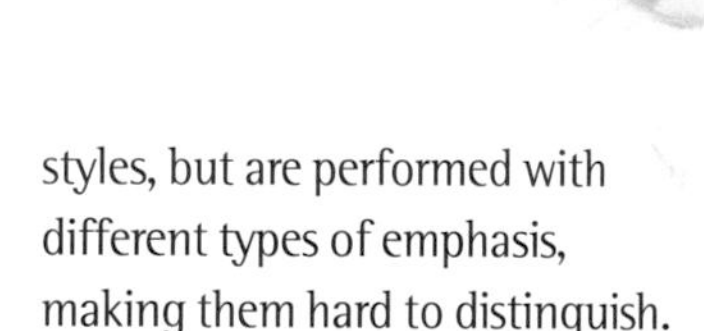

variations and similarities

Specific movements from one style can be identified in each of the other styles, but are performed with different types of emphasis, making them hard to distinguish.

There are also a number of subdivisions of each of the five major styles of tai chi, reflecting the fact that methods and teachings differ from one school to the next. Although a number of new styles of tai chi have been introduced in recent years, they are all variations on the same general theme with their roots going back to the original tai chi form developed some 300 years ago.

The practice of any one of the five styles takes years of dedicated study—it has even been said that a lifetime's experience can rarely give complete mastery of the art, although years of practice certainly provide a great sense of accomplishment.

Tai chi may be described as the physical, mental, and spiritual embodiment of all that exists between Heaven and Earth.

health

It is quite common for people to impose personal limitations on themselves—both psychological and physical—that inhibit their capabilities and personal growth. So, instead of thinking positively and channeling our energy to achieve the best results, we find reasons not to succeed in various aspects of life and become attached to the negative beliefs that stunt our progress. Tai chi theory asserts that we can surpass these self-limitations by adapting our mental outlook. The student of tai chi is taught to look beyond the simplicity of its movements and encouraged to explore their internal senses, thoughts, and feelings—and ultimately to realize

HOW TAI CHI IMPROVES YOUR HEALTH

How can tai chi improve our health? In China, tai chi is regularly prescribed to assist the recovery of hospital patients and has been proved to positively affect chronic diseases, including high blood pressure, tuberculosis, and respiratory disorders. There are a wide range of general and specific health benefits to be gained from the practice of tai chi. Listing them all would be a mammoth task, but if reduced to its core components the technique can be divided into three clear fundamental principles, each revolving around calm and balance. The three principles work together to regulate and control your being:

1 regulate the body

Tai chi teaches the body "good habits." It aligns the joints correctly, gently exercises the muscles without strain, and massages the internal organs to maximize efficiency.

2 regulate the breath

Correct diaphragmatic breathing stimulates the organs from within the body. It optimizes oxygen intake and efficiently expels toxin-laden air.

3 regulate the mind

By concentrating the mind, we focus the spirit. All actions require thought on some level, and because the mind controls our actions, we can use it to improve all other aspects of ourselves.

Only through the correct practice of these three components can you discover the real secrets of tai chi. Of the three options, the easiest first experience of tai chi is regulation of the body through physical movements, and this alone can offer significant rewards.

Young children have boundless energy and spirit, and yet as they grow and develop, this natural inner energy starts to diminish. We become accustomed to shallow breathing, we rely more on our physical muscles, and in most cases we live unhealthy lifestyles. Overflowing with practical concerns, our minds are constantly active and this contributes to tension and stress.

the endless creativity of the human mind. You may think this sounds beyond your reach; but the question to ask yourself is, "Why not?" Every human being has similar capabilities, and differences arise mainly through the limitations that we place on ourselves.

relaxation

As with most arts, tai chi takes practice and perseverance. A teacher will often simply ask their pupil to relax, but even this requires a certain amount of practice, as such an instruction is not confined to the muscles. In Chinese, the term "relax" means literally "sink down" and is applied to the mind, the breath, and the body. The breathing method advocated by tai chi practitioners is similar to that of children when in a deep sleep. If we look at resting children, we see that the breath is drawn deep into the stomach, "sinking" to the center of the body so that the muscles rest and become heavy.

The practice of tai chi uses healing and revitalization, and this starts with relaxed, controlled movements to invigorate the body. Tai chi can be thought of as active relaxation, and the more you practice the more it can be used in your daily life.

Great things are often achieved through the simplest means. The profound benefits experienced through regular tai chi practice may be attributed quite simply to moving, breathing, and concentration.

2

getting started

When starting your tai chi practice, you need to consider how to prepare for your session. This chapter examines how to prepare mentally by choosing an appropriate environment and suitable clothing. It then shows you how to warm up properly, working your way around your body, before looking at "qigong," the practice of balancing the body's energy through concentrating the mind and breath.

beginning your practice

When learning the art of tai chi, you should prepare yourself mentally to understand what lies ahead. Start by identifying your own particular habits when learning something new. Do you usually start off enthusiastically and then abandon your efforts in preference to the next interesting project? Have you ever successfully developed a new skill and continued to use it? Or do your efforts tend to be half-hearted, lacking a real drive to succeed? If you understand the patterns of your past behavior that have prevented you from achieving, then you can strive to avoid repeating those patterns. Similarly, if you have previously developed a new skill, then use the positive patterns that enabled you to succeed. Tai chi takes time, effort, and patience. Without these three elements, your journey will be far less rewarding and much more challenging.

gradual progression

A common mistake with any new venture is trying to learn too fast. Remember that, depending on the individual student, it can take anywhere from a month to a year or more to learn the form. Don't be afraid to take your time. It is better to spend a year reaching a good standard than to have learned the entire form badly in just six weeks. Although we all learn at different rates and with different results, as a general rule each movement should be learned and practiced every day for a week. In this way, the technique will be built up gradually until the whole form is complete. Try to use the goal of learning one move every week so that you are more likely to succeed. The program at the back of the book provides a general practice schedule, which will enable you to reach the end of the form successfully.

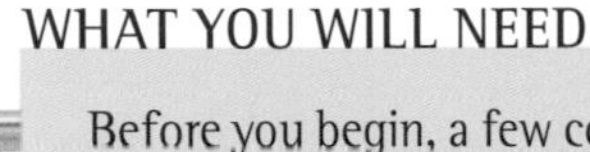

WHAT YOU WILL NEED

Before you begin, a few considerations will make your practice sessions run more smoothly.

be aware of your surroundings

1

Beginners often prefer to practice in the privacy of their home or backyard, away from the curious eyes of onlookers. However, there are many distractions in the home, such as the telephone, the television, pets, and food. Aim to avoid these distractions by using a quiet part of the day, maybe in the morning, in the early evening, or at dusk; eating an hour or so before your practice so you won't feel hungry; switching the phone to "silent" mode; and practicing away from pets and family members.

The best place to practice is in a natural environment. If the weather allows, go outside where the air is fresh and you can hear natural sounds such as birds singing, streams trickling, and trees rustling in the wind. The early morning provides the freshest air. Find a quiet corner in a park where it is not too busy.

wear suitable clothing

2

Your muscles should feel as though they have room to stretch and flex—loose clothing allows the skin to breathe and lets the body move without restriction. Avoid tight-fitting clothes that hug your body.

let your feet feel the earth

3

Shoes with thick soles give a sense of separation from the supporting ground below. Avoid such shoes; you need to feel in close contact with the earth. The Chinese generally practice in thin-soled shoes or slippers to more effectively use the energy of the immense mass of the Earth. Although the idea of exercising in bare feet may be appealing, it is considered more fitting to wear shoes for tai chi.

warming up

It is important before exercise of any kind to warm up correctly. Although tai chi is a gentle form of exercise, it should still be preceded by a light loosening of the joints. This can be done simply by slowly rotating the joints one by one. In tai chi, you should be constantly mindful of the movements being performed, and this also applies to the warm-up. When rotating the wrists, for example, concentrate on attaining the greatest range of motion possible—you should literally feel the joint loosening and warming.

To ensure that no joints are forgotten, work methodically from the top of the body down to the toes. It is important to avoid undue stress to the joints, so the utmost care must be taken when warming the neck and knees, because they are very delicate and can be easily damaged.

WARMING UP

1 general warm-up

Stand with your feet apart and your hands on your hips. Imagine a silver cord attached from the sky to the top of your head toward the back. This position stretches the backbone and should be maintained throughout every stage of your exercise.

Many exercise regimens have a specific number of repetitions for each particular movement, so the following instructions are intended only as a guide. The practitioner may repeat a posture as much or as little as feels comfortable.

2 head and neck

Gently but firmly turn the head to face the left. Turn as fully as possible without overstraining. Repeat to the right. Then look down to the floor without letting your ears move forward. Then look up toward the sky as if you are stretching the chin as far away from the shoulders as possible. Return to the forward position.

Next, tilt the head to the left as if trying to touch the ear to the shoulder. Repeat to the right. Do the whole exercise twice. This exercise dispenses with the need for neck rotations, which can cause discomfort. Whenever moving the neck, it is common practice to stretch up to lengthen the spine. This improves posture and reduces headaches and neck-related problems.

3 shoulders

Rest the arms to the sides. Rotate the shoulders in a forward direction using the largest range of motion that is comfortable. Repeat this exercise eight times forward and eight times backward. The motion should be held for a fraction longer when the shoulders are as far back as possible. This encourages the surrounding muscles to relax.

WARMING UP continued

elbows

Raise the arms to the left and right sides so that the arms form one straight line. Keep the elbows still and rotate both arms inward like the propellers of an airplane. Repeat the exercise eight times inward and eight times outward.

wrists

Clasp the hands together and interlock the fingers. Keeping the palms in contact, rotate the wrists eight times in both directions. After 16 rotations, separate and vigorously shake both hands.

hips

Rub the hands briskly together until they feel warm and place them on the kidney region of the back. Keep the feet and head still while rotating the hips in a large circle. Repeat four times in each direction.

waist

With the feet shoulder width apart, let the arms hang freely at the sides. Turn the waist from side to side and allow the arms to follow until a good rhythm is found. Let the arms swing in time with the waist movement, gently striking the body at the end of each turn. This should be repeated at least 36 times.

knees 1

To effectively warm the knees without strain, stand on one leg to rotate the free leg. Standing with the feet together while rotating both knees is a popular method, but this can cause twisting, especially in older practitioners. Standing on one leg not only avoids this, but also improves balance, strength, and limb control.

knees 2

The alternative method is to stand with the feet almost together (allowing a two-finger-width gap between them) and gently rotate the knees in a circular motion. Keep the hands just above the kneecaps, but do not support your weight on the arms. Do not rotate to the fullest degree, because this may cause discomfort. Repeat four times in each direction.

ankles and toes

With the feet apart, place the ball of one foot on the ground and rotate the ankle around it in a broad motion. This will exercise both the ankle joint and all the toes. Rotate eight times in each direction, and repeat for the other foot.

hamstrings

With the feet still shoulder-width apart, slowly lean forward, bending from the hips. Continue to bend until you feel a stretching sensation in the back of the legs and calves. Be sure not to arch the back at any point. Slowly return to the upright position. To help keep the back straight, look up at the start of the movement and maintain the neck position throughout. You should not perform this exercise if you suffer from any kind of back condition.

finally

Conclude the warm-up by shaking the arms, wrists, fingers, ankles, and legs.

qigong

Qigong (pronounced "chee gong") is the practice of balancing the body's energy, or chi, by concentrating the mind and breath. Spelled numerous ways—such as "chi gong," "chi kung,"

QUIET STANDING

Try to follow the four points listed below and opposite and incorporate qigong into your tai chi practice.

1. Stand with your feet shoulder width apart and your arms resting by the sides. Your knees should be straight but not locked and your spine stretched up toward the sky. The back of your neck should be stretched as though a single cord were suspending the back of your head from above. Your chest and back are relaxed.

2. Place your tongue softly on the palate behind the top teeth, and use your diaphragm to gently draw the breath in and out of your body without allowing the chest cavity to rise or fall.

and "ki-gong"—it is a popular practice among tai chi practitioners and usually follows the warm-up. There are many methods of qigong. For the beginner, there is a simple method called "quiet standing," a term that encompasses a number of simple qigong exercises. Although the simplest methods are sometimes the hardest to perform, they will offer valuable rewards to those who master them.

Your mind needs to be relaxed. This is difficult until you are familiar with the forms, but persevere and you will find the right focus.

3

With qigong, you must keep your mind clear. This can be a tough challenge for the beginner, so an effective technique is to focus your mind on an area called the "dan tien," positioned at approximately three fingers width below the navel and a third of the way into the body. This area is said to store the body's vital energy. Imagine a small yellow ball of light about the size of a fist located at the dan tien. As you inhale, feel this ball marginally expand. As you exhale, feel it return to the size of a fist. Giving your mind a focus is an effective way to reduce stress and to cultivate stillness. The color yellow is significant here because it represents energy, well-being, activity, and life.

4

Although the body remains motionless, the mind is actively calming. You should eventually find that other intruding thoughts will fade and any muscular tension will ebb away. Although the exercise is simple, distractions can at first make it difficult to stand for any length of time. Build up your perseverance by initially standing for about 10 minutes at a time until it becomes fairly easy; then increase the duration by 5-minute increments until you have achieved 30 minutes. Once you can stand comfortably for 30–60 minutes, you have achieved the maximum benefit from this exercise.

3

practice essentials

This chapter introduces the fundamentals of tai chi practice. It examines each part of the body—the torso, the back, the shoulders, and the waist—and looks at how they should be treated during your session. It then introduces the nine stances and three hand positions commonly used in all tai chi movements.

fundamentals

1

THE TORSO

The torso forms the foundation of the structure and carriage of the human frame. Any changes in the alignment of the torso will have a direct effect on the entire body. Good alignment is paramount to the development of the tai chi practitioner.

2

THE BACK

Relax as much as possible and make a mental note of how your muscles feel. Now lean forward slightly, and be aware of any changes in the muscle tension through your body. Return to the upright posture, and you should feel the release of excess tension in your mid-back to your lower back. Repeat the exercise by leaning backward, and you will feel the changes in tension through your abdomen.

- Maintaining a correct posture will avoid tension in the back, which will tighten the muscles and pull on the vertebrae. When this happens, other muscles try to compensate by pulling back. This usually causes a zigzag of tension throughout the back that leads to unnecessary discomfort. Being straight and being upright are not the same thing. A pole, for example, is straight, but not necessarily upright. It is possible for it to be both, but one does not automatically result in the other. The same applies to the spine. The movements in the 24-step form, with a few exceptions, require your back to be both straight and upright.

- Although the spine is naturally curved, we can assume it to be approximately straight.

- When upright, the vertebrae that make up your spine balance on top of each other. This means that the muscles surrounding the torso are free from strain.

3

THE SHOULDERS

Your shoulders should always be relaxed and soft; it sounds simple, but it is actually quite hard to achieve. Even after several years of study, students still need to be reminded to drop their shoulders. Be sure not to slouch the shoulders forward because this will restrict the cavity around the heart. One method of releasing tension in the shoulders is to squeeze the shoulder blades together for about five seconds. This activates the postural muscles between the blades, allowing the top of the shoulders to relax.

4

THE WAIST

Although the body is mostly kept upright, tai chi does require the waist to be flexible and mobile, particularly when changing from one position to the next. In terms of its martial applications, the effective use of the waist will always improve the chances of success. Most strikes involve the arms and legs, with the waist initiating the power of the movement. This can be likened to a hammer driving a nail—the head of the hammer is the active component, but it is the handle that provides the power. In much the same way, a punch or kick is more effective when powered from the waist.

- Many exercise regimens concentrate on the external body, with the emphasis on toning the body, tightening the muscles, and trimming away fat. Tai chi, however, focuses on the use of the internal organs to achieve a state of well-being. Think of a glass of water. Add a few spoonfuls of salt, and allow it to sink to the bottom. If the top portion of the mixture were stirred, just a small portion of the salt would mix and the overall effect would be minimal. If the bottom section were stirred, the whole solution would be affected. The lower portion of the water represents the waist, so turning the waist exercises and stimulates all internal organs, resulting in improved health.

fundamentals: stances 1

These positions refer to the final placement of the legs in any given posture. There are five main stances in the 24-step form. The knee and toes of each leg should always point in the same direction, to correctly align the joints and prevent unnecessary strain.

bow stance

In this posture (sometimes called the "Forward Stance") the front leg is bent with the knee over the toes and the back leg is straight but not locked. The front toes point directly ahead, while the back toes point out at 45 degrees. This stance should feel reasonably comfortable. If you look down your front leg, your knee should obstruct the view of your toes.

empty step

The Empty Step is so called because the front leg is devoid of weight and is therefore "empty." All body weight rests on the back leg, which, as in the Bow Stance, is angled at 45 degrees. The front foot points forward and rests on either the ball of the foot or the heel, depending on the technique. If held for even a few seconds, the back thigh should start to ache. If it does not ache, your spine may be incorrectly bent either forward or backward, therefore releasing pressure from the leg. This is an incorrect position and exerts undue stress on the back.

side step

The Side Step opens and closes the form and occurs during the Cloud Hands movement. It is a simple stance that requires only that the toes point forward. When lifting the foot, the heel leaves the ground first followed by the toes. When stepping, the toes touch the ground first, followed by the heel. The widest distance between the feet in the Side Step is two shoulder widths. When at their closest, the feet are about one fist width apart.

single leg

As its name implies, the Single Leg stance involves standing on one leg. The support leg is angled at around 45 degrees, while the "hanging" leg faces directly ahead, with the knee lifted to waist height and the toes pointing to the floor. This stance improves balance and strength.

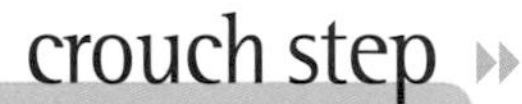

crouch step

The Crouch Step is a demanding stance, and is found in the latter half of the form. It starts with the feet three shoulder widths apart, with both toes angled at 45 degrees to each corner. One leg bears most of the weight with the knee bent, while the body sinks down toward the ground. The other leg is almost straight. Both feet remain flat on the floor.

fundamentals: stances 2

stepping

Stepping is the transitional means through which we change from one posture to the next. The final position of a particular movement must be backed by a well-structured step. It may be compared to throwing a punch: the final position may be correct, but without correct execution of the technique, it is of little use.

half step

All Half Steps are in a forward direction. When a Half Step is taken from a Bow Stance, the back foot travels half the distance between the feet. Once the weight is on the back leg, the front foot is free to step forward onto the toe or heel as required.

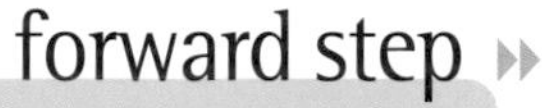

forward step

The "slip-heel" Forward Step is used to advance from one Bow Stance to another. Sit halfway back and turn the front foot out by 90 degrees. Step forward with the back leg, passing by the supporting ankle. Step first onto the heel before placing the toes down. Slide the back heel backward by 45 degrees. Depending on flexibility, when turning the front foot the practitioner may turn up to 90 degrees.

backward step »

With the Backward Step, the toes always land before the heel and the front foot should pass close to the supporting ankle on its way back. At the end of the step, the front heel adjusts so that the toes point straight ahead. The feet should have about one fist width between them. It is acceptable for the length of a Backward Step to be marginally shorter than a Forward Step, although the difference should not be marked.

HAND POSTURES

In the Yang style of tai chi, there are three hand shapes to learn. By far the most common is the Open Palm; considered to be the most versatile shape, it easily adapts to any other shape, whether to grip, punch, push, or guide. The Fist and Hook Hand are less commonly used, but should also be familiar movements.

1 the fist

To form the tai chi Fist, imagine gripping a pencil with each finger wrapped gently around it. Your thumb should lightly support your index finger. In other martial arts, the fist is usually clenched tight as if it were squeezing the pencil. In tai chi, the Fist is formed but holds no tension. The Fist is used twice in the form, once in Box Tiger's Ears and once in Deflect, Parry, and Punch. When punching, the wrist is usually straight so that the back of the hand lies on the same plane as the forearm. However, in Box Tiger's Ears the wrists are slightly flexed, as if slightly revving the throttle of a motorbike.

2 the open palm

The Open Palm is the dominant hand shape throughout the form. The hand is held open with fingers and thumb gently splayed as if waving goodbye to a friend. The Open Palm should be well formed, but not stiff. This hand shape is sometimes referred to as Willow Leaf Palm, because it resembles a large leaf and is slightly concave in shape.

3 the hook hand

The Hook Hand is formed by lightly pinching the tips of your fingers around the tip of your thumb. The correct shape can be achieved by holding—or imagining that you are holding—the wide end of an egg in your palm while the fingers and thumb surround it and meet at the top. This hand shape represents the gripping of an opponent's arm, or even a strike using the back of the wrist. The Hook Hand occurs in two forms throughout the sequence, Single Whip and Snake Creeps Down. Each form is performed once to the left and once to the right. In each case the wrist is bent as if the fingers are aiming toward the elbow.

4

the forms

Put theory into practice with the following 24-step Beijing short form. This chapter illustrates each form with step-by-step illustrations and captions, demonstrates how each key movement should be performed, and gives hints and tips on improving your practice. It also identifies common pitfalls relating to the back, the waist, the shoulders, the arms, the legs, the head and neck, and the hips.

background

A sequence of movements in tai chi that follows a specific order is known as a "form," but it can also be described as a "routine," "sequence," "set," or "step." A single posture within a sequence can also be called a "form." The 24-step routine featured here is referred to as the "short form," the "24-steps," or the "simplified form."

The 24-step routine is a standardized sequence, meaning that each of its postures is specifically numbered and classified. A short excerpt from the form will often contain several movements that are counted as a single move. Deflect, Parry, and Punch (see pp. 76–77) is one example—it appears to be three movements, but is counted as one. The entire 24-step form should take about five minutes to perform from beginning to end. The form is practiced at an even pace with fluid, continuous movements and no obvious pauses.

standing height

There are three positional heights to use when practicing the form. The first is Standing Height, when the body is at its tallest, such as in the opening forms (see pp. 38–39) and Closing Form (see pp. 80–81). A standing posture is also used during a kicking movement when the support leg is straight.

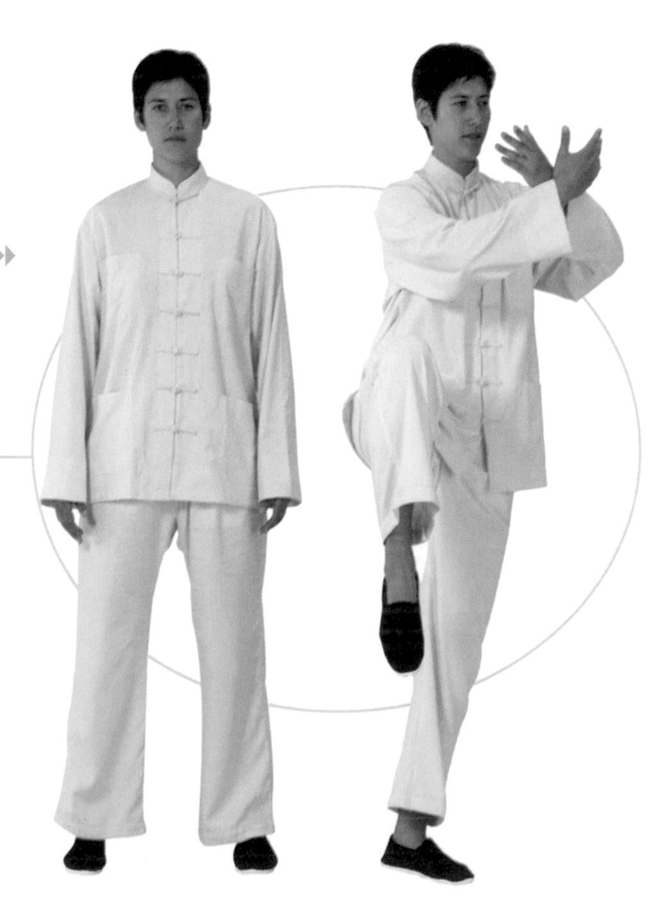

what to expect

As you practice, you will become aware of subtle changes in your body—your legs should become stronger, your balance more stable, and your outlook more focused. You should also feel more confident, more relaxed, and better able to deal with tension and stress. This strengthening process will be a gradual transformation. You will start to find that any activities that have presented problems in the past and that you might have been avoiding may be resumed and built up gradually. Your fitness level will increase, you will be less vulnerable to injury, and the signs of aging will recede. All these benefits can be gained through regular practice, which will instill in you good body mechanics and posture.

As you progress with tai chi, you will feel subtle new sensations throughout your body. Your hands will feel "full" and charged; your feet will feel rooted and firm. A sense of relaxed strength enters the body and the mind becomes focused. You may even complete the form having felt "absent" for part of it. These are all indications of progress.

mid height

The second position is Mid Height, used in stances when the feet are separated and one or both legs are bent, such as in the Bow Stance and Empty

Step (see p. 26). This level is roughly 8 in. (20 cm) lower than Standing Height and is most commonly maintained in Yang-style forms.

low level

The third height is Low Level, when the body is dropped into a more difficult posture, such as that used in Snake Creeps Down (see pp. 68–71). When first learning, it is advisable to stay at Mid Height or Standing Height until your body becomes more familiar with the form.

form structure theory

In simple terms, the ancient Chinese Han philosophy explains that existence started from a single point in time and space, or a single principle called the Tao. This point then divided into two parts of separate principles—represented by "yin" and "yang." The interplay of these two opposing forces then brought about all things that exist in the universe. It assumes that all things will return to just two forces, and eventually to one single point. The tai chi form mirrors this process.

On the pages that follow, the first section (stages 1–6) introduces the three basic steps of tai chi—Forward Stepping, Half Stepping, and Backward Stepping, in combination with the Open Hand Palm or Willow Leaf Palm shape (see p. 29). The second section (stages 7–12) contains the four fundamental principles of Ward Off (*pung*), Roll Back (*lu*), Squeeze (*ji*), and Press (*an*), as well as Side Stepping. The third section (stages 13–18) represents the more challenging part of the routine. The balance and limb control established in the first two sections will now be tested with the inclusion of two Heel Kicks. Hip flexibility and leg strength are both challenged during Snake Creeps Down (see pp. 68–71), and the direction of stepping now deviates from a straight line. Another relatively demanding section, the fourth one (stages 19–24), brings the sequence to a close.

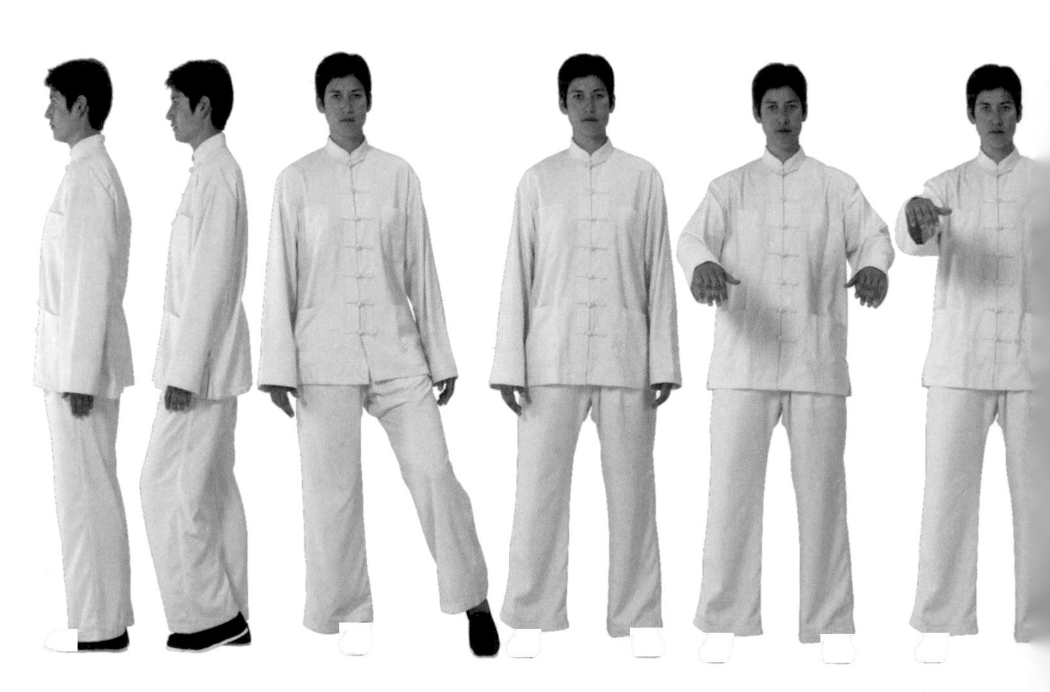

FORMS THAT INTRODUCE THE THREE BASIC STEPS

1 Starting Position

The form starts simply with feet together and hands to the sides, a position of balance and unity. This is used in preparation for the separation of the feet, representing the division of unity into yin and yang.

2 Part the Wild Horse's Mane

Stepping first to the left (yin, which is soft, passive, and relaxed) and then to the right (yang, which is strong, light, and hot), Part the Wild Horse's Mane dictates that the left hand is forward when the left leg is forward, and the right hand is forward when the right leg is forward. This represents the simplest principle to start the form.

3 White Crane Spreads Wings

This provides a transition from one principle to another. Here we see a change to an Empty Step (see p. 26) with neither hand prominent. One hand is high to the left, while the other is low to the right. This can be seen as a balanced position using the opposites of high and low, left and right, and yin and yang. The change relates to the movement of the prominent hand.

4 Brush Knee and Twist Step

This technique requires that when one leg is forward, the opposite hand is forward.

5 Strum the Lute

This is another transitional posture. Although the weight falls on the back leg, the arms are no longer neutral. Both arms are poised in front of the body—with one high and one low. This position changes the dynamic of yin and yang.

6 Repulse the Monkey

This transition is the precursor to a new idea—Backward Stepping. In Repulse the Monkey, we see the reverse of Brush Knee and Twist Step, which carries the weight forward, maintains width between the feet, and keeps the opposite hand in front with the body advancing and approximately square. In Repulse the Monkey, the weight is backward, there is no width between the feet, the same hand is forward, and the body is retreating and angled.

7 Cross Hands and Closing Form

Starting in section two, the study of the form becomes more complex until the final stages, where the Cross Hands position reveals a symmetrical ordered shape with the feet once again divided into the balanced forces of yin and yang. To close the routine, the arms separate and rest at the sides, as if in a calming state, and the feet once again come together in unity.

working through the forms

There may be subtle differences between the following photographs that illustrate the moves and the text that explains them. In these cases, the photograph offers a simplified method suitable for the novice, and the explanatory text provides greater detail. The latter may also be used to further refine the form. Feel free to practice at any time of day, although mornings provide the freshest, least polluted air. Start by choosing a quiet location, avoid possible interruptions, and give yourself time to relax. Before you begin, it can be helpful to place markers on each corner and wall denoting the appropriate directions. Start by establishing which direction is forward—this will then represent the front (see below).

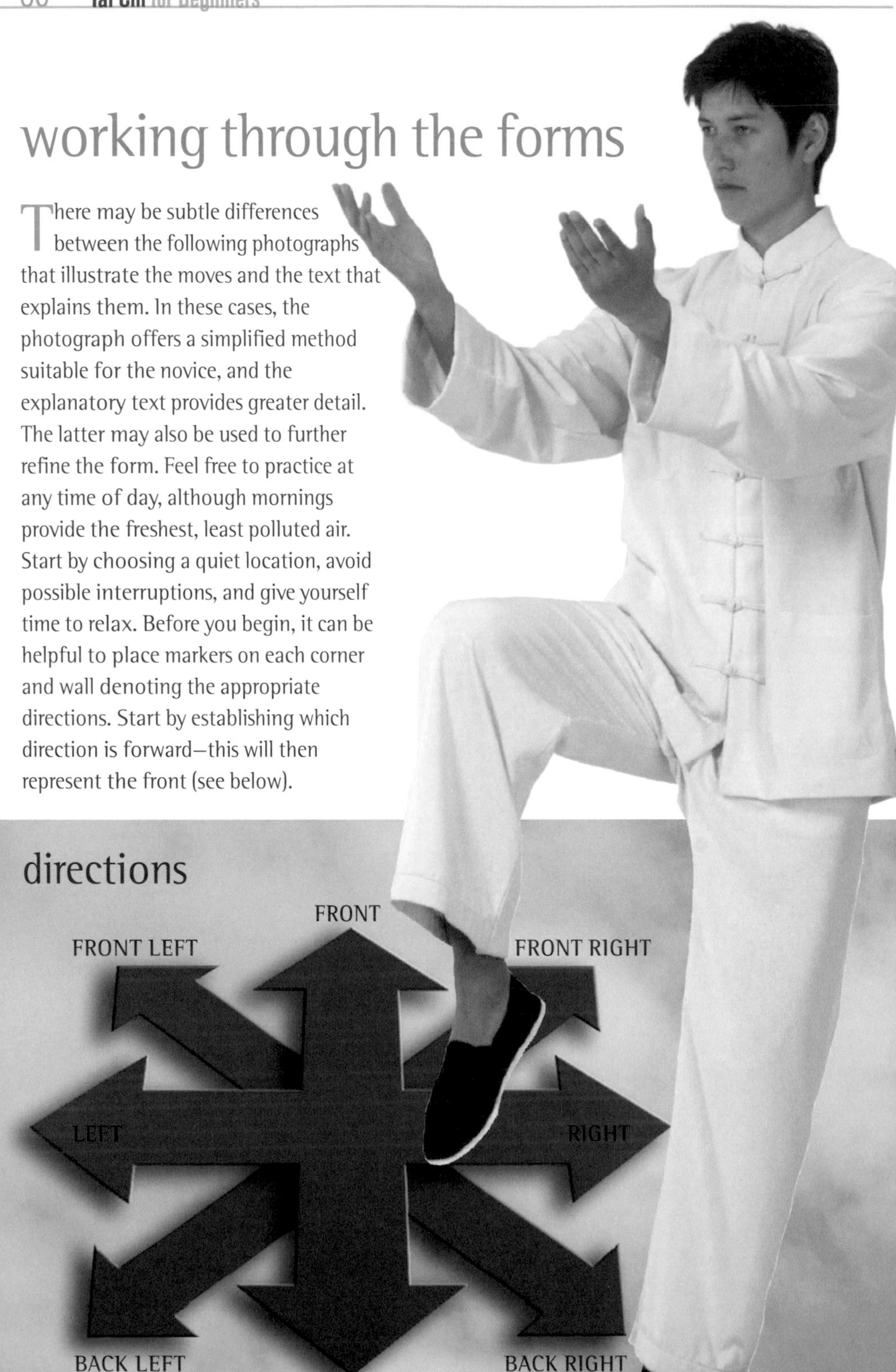

FORM OVERVIEW

SECTION 1

	Preparation Step
1	Regulate the Breath Hold the Ball (transitional link)
2	Part the Wild Horse's Mane (both sides)
3	White Crane Spreads Wings
4	Brush Knee and Twist Step (both sides)
5	Strum the Lute
6	Repulse the Monkey

SECTION 2

7	Grasp the Peacock's Tail (left side)
8	Grasp the Peacock's Tail (right side)
9	Single Whip
10	Hands Like Clouds
11	Single Whip
12	High Pat on Horse

SECTION 3

13	Separate and Heel Kick (right side)
14	Box Tiger's Ears (transitional turn)
15	Separate and Heel Kick (left side)
16	Snake Creeps Down and Golden Rooster Stands On One Leg (left side)
17	Snake Creeps Down and Golden Rooster Stands On One Leg (right side)
18	Fair Lady Works the Shuttles (both sides)

SECTION 4

19	Needle at Sea Bottom
20	Fan Through Back
21	Deflect, Parry, and Punch
22	Apparent Close Up
23	Cross Hands
24	Closing Form

forms 1–6

The opening forms introduce the three basic steps of tai chi—Forward Stepping, Half Stepping, and Backward Stepping. They also contain the predominant hand posture, the Open Palm, or Willow Leaf Palm.

FORM PREPARATION STEP

Stand with your feet together and your arms resting by your sides. Lift the left heel followed by the toes and step to the left. Place the left foot at shoulder-width distance from the right foot (putting your toes down first). This simple step will mentally prepare you for the Regulate the Breath exercise ahead.

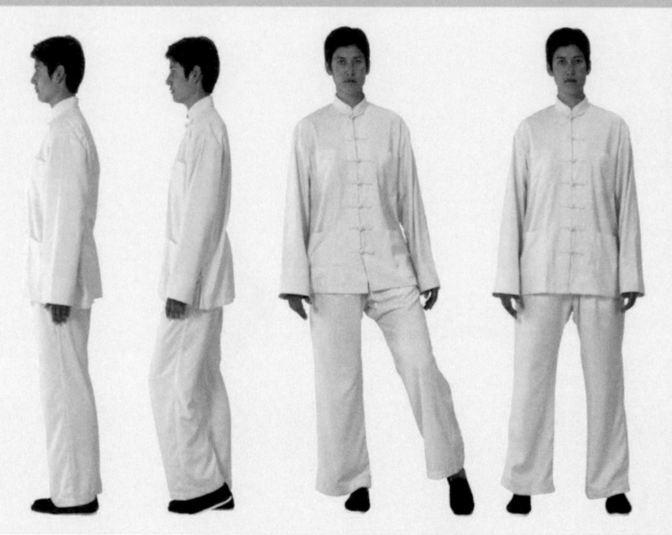

FORM 1 HOLD THE BALL (TRANSITIONAL LINK)

Shift your body weight to your right leg, turn your waist about 20 degrees to the right, and separate your hands. When your weight is fully to the right, turn your whole body to face the front left corner. Raise your right hand and lower your left hand into position, while also resting your left foot by your right ankle.

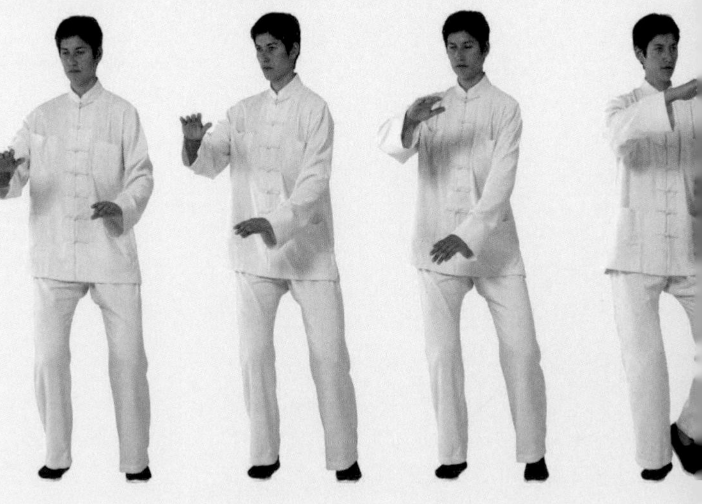

how's it going?

This is the first movement in the 24-step sequence and incorporates the Regulate the Breath exercise. The movement is slow and concentrated, and lifting your arms is accompanied by an inhale (in-breath). Sinking your body is coordinated with an out-breath. You must take care not to incline your body, grip your toes to the floor, or let your hands become either left- or right-biased. Also, try not to lean forward at any time during the posture.

how's it going?

REGULATE THE BREATH

Raise both arms slowly in front of your body to shoulder height, keeping your arms and wrists straight. Once at shoulder height, bend your knees and elbows simultaneously while keeping your back upright. Continue this downward motion until your elbows lie just in front of your body with your hands at about waist height.

PART THE WILD HORSE'S MANE (BOTH SIDES)

Step your left leg toward the left wall, transferring your weight smoothly to the left. As your left hand lifts, your right hand sinks to the right hip. Your left hand finishes at face height. Remember to also slip the back heel.

form 2 (continued) ▸▸

1

forms 1–6 continued

This movement is fairly simple and can be likened to throwing a Frisbee. The main characteristic is that the front arm and corresponding leg both end up facing forward.

FORM 2

PART THE WILD HORSE'S MANE (BOTH SIDES) CONTINUED

RIGHT SIDE
Sit back on your right leg and turn your left toes to face the back right corner. As you bring your right leg to meet your left, form the Hold the Ball position (see p. 38) with your left hand up and your right hand down.

Now step forward with your right leg, transferring your weight smoothly. As your right hand lifts, your left hand should sink to your left side and settle by the hips. Again, your right hand is at face height with the palm gently twisting up.

how's it going?

Be sure to keep your back straight and upright throughout, and do not bias your hips to either side while stepping forward. Also, make sure that your weight transfers smoothly from leg to leg.

how's it going?

LEFT SIDE
Sit back on your left leg and turn your right toes to the front left corner. As you bring your left leg in to meet your right, form the Hold the Ball position (see p. 38) with your right hand up and left hand down. Step forward with your left leg, transferring the weight smoothly. As your left hand lifts, your right hand should sink to your right hip. Again, your left hand should be at face height.

forms 1–6 continued

This is the first movement with a Half Step and is especially useful in strengthening the legs and testing balance. Your movements should be small and controlled.

FORM 3 WHITE CRANE SPREADS WINGS

Without moving your front foot, take a Half Step forward with your right foot with the toes on the ground and the heel off the floor.

Turn your body simultaneously to the left back corner and form the Hold the Ball posture with the left hand held high.

Then, raise your right hand up and across to the right, placing the right heel on the ground. At this point, the weight is entirely on the back foot, the back of the right palm is parallel to the front wall, and the left-hand fingers are pointing to the right wrist.

how's it going?

While looking directly forward at eye level, keep your left and right hand in your peripheral vision. The left shoulder will try to lift, so keep it relaxed. Do not put any weight on the front foot.

how's it going?

Your body should now be facing the front left corner. Turn your body to face the left wall, lowering your left hand down and across the body to rest at your left side in line with the knee. Keep the right hand in the same place. Now step your left foot gently forward by no more than 12 in. (30 cm) until your knee is almost straight and the ball of the foot touches the floor.

You should now be in the Empty Step (see p. 26). The final picture above shows the view as seen from the front wall.

form 4 ▸▸

1

forms 1–6 continued

Unlike previous postures, this one ends with the opposing hand and leg facing forward. It is repeated three times and introduces the idea of "twisting" power. This form uses large circular movements of the arms.

FORM 4 BRUSH KNEE AND TWIST STEP (BOTH SIDES)

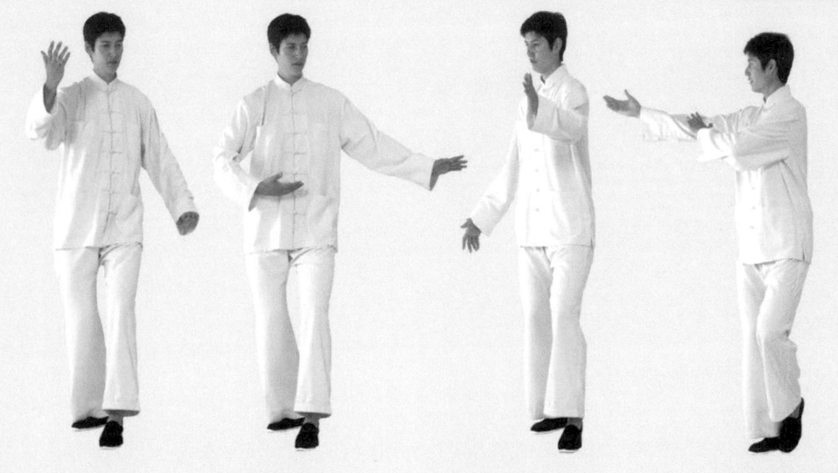

Turn the waist toward the left. As you turn back to face the left wall, lower the right hand to your "dan tien" (see p. 21), palm facing up. The left hand lifts toward the left back corner, palm facing up. Bring the left leg back to hover by the right foot. Straighten the

This hand should be level with the dan tien. Bend the right arm so that the thumb points to the right ear. As you form a left Bow Stance, the left hand traces a line around the left knee. Push the right-hand fingers forward until almost at the end of their

how's it going?

Students tend to straighten the pushing arm and incline the back one forward—this should be avoided. The lower hand should rest in line with the front knee with the palm facing the floor. The forward hand should be in line with the corresponding shoulder.

how's it going?

right arm at the same time to point to the right wall, palm up.

The left arm travels in a slight upward arc from the left back corner to

the right front corner, resting by the right elbow, palm down.

As the left heel steps forward, press the left hand down.

length. The wrist should gently flex back. To change sides,

sit back and turn the left toes to point to the back left corner, and

mirror the first side (as shown in front wall perspective). To finish

the third Brush Knee, simply repeat the first once again.

form 5 ▸▸

1

forms 1–6 continued

Here, we adopt the second Half Step of section one. Unlike the first, this posture requires the heel to touch the floor, to represent a kick or trip. Most of your weight will end up on your back leg.

FORM 5 STRUM THE LUTE

Take a Half Step forward with the right leg, gently extending the right hand.

Lift the left hand to the back left corner with the palm facing down.

As you sit back on the right heel, turn both palms to face downward.

The right toes should point to the front left corner and both hands should be at shoulder height.

how's it going?

In the final position, it is tempting to put weight on your front foot. To check if this is happening, lift the front leg off the floor without moving the body. If your body doesn't move, the weight is correct. Maintain a small gap under your arms.

▲how's it going?

Lift the left leg and place the heel toward the left wall. At the same time, draw the elbows toward the body so that the left palm faces the front left corner and the right palm faces the back left corner.

The fingers of your right hand should point toward your left elbow.

The left-hand fingertips are level with the eyes and the body should face the front left corner.

1

forms 1–6 continued

Although the general practice of tai chi reduces signs of aging, Repulse the Monkey is the only sequence said to specifically slow time, as the steps are all retreating. The Backward Step is also said to calm the chatter of the brain.

FORM 6 REPULSE THE MONKEY

Lower the right hand to the waist (palm facing up). Continue to draw an arc up to the front right corner and turn the left palm upward. The left leg begins its backward step in time with the right hand.

To change sides, lift the left hand to the back right corner and extend the right hand toward the left wall. Then turn both palms to face upward, and as you step back with the right foot the left arm should bend and travel toward the right wrist.

how's it going?

As in the Brush Knee technique, do not allow the elbows to travel behind the shoulders at any time. Backward Steps are as bold as Forward Steps, and should not be shortened.

how's it going?

As your left leg steps back onto the ball of the foot, the right arm bends, moving forward until it is above the left wrist. As your body weight sinks onto the left leg, the right heel turns in, and the left hand draws back to the dan tien. The body faces the back left corner.

As the weight transfers fully to the right leg, the left hand gently pushes and the right hand draws back to the dan tien. Straighten the left heel to complete the step.

The Repulse the Monkey form should be repeated twice more. The third time should be identical to the first, except that the left toes are down instead of the heel, and the fourth is identical to the second.

2 forms 7–12

There is no stepping in this short sequence. Instead, the shifting of the weight from one foot to the other is emphasized, along with the turning of the waist. Try to keep the pelvis level during the form.

FORM 7 GRASP THE PEACOCK'S TAIL (LEFT SIDE)

To Ward Off, draw an arc with the right arm to the front wall at shoulder height, bring the left foot back into a T-step, and use a Hold the Ball position with the right hand high. Step with the left leg to the left wall and lift the left arm up. At the same time, lower the right

Your right palm should face up. Draw your hands down toward your waist and bring the weight to the back leg. Continue the motion of your arms to point toward the front wall. To Squeeze, turn your waist back to face the left wall while your

how's it going?

As the front toe lifts during Press, a common error is to straighten and lock the front knee. This reduces forward power, and is strongly discouraged. Be sure to distinguish between Part the Wild Horse's Mane and Ward Off.

how's it going?

hand past the left wrist and down to the right hip. The final arm

movements should be coordinated by turning the right heel.

To Roll Back, turn the waist slightly to the left, at the same time

turning both palms so that the left palm faces down.

right hand faces the left wrist. As the weight transfers

to the left leg, gently squeeze your right palm against

your left wrist and extend your hands forward to form a

circle out in front of your chest.

forms 7 (continued) and 8 ▸▸

2 forms 7–12 continued

This form consists of four main movements: Ward Off (*pung*), Roll Back (*lu*), Squeeze (*ji*), and Press (*an*). These four movements are of paramount importance in all tai chi styles.

FORM 7 GRASP THE PEACOCK'S TAIL (LEFT SIDE) CONTINUED

To Press, keep the weight forward, and separate the arms until they are parallel at shoulder height, with the palms facing down. Sit back and lift the left toes while bringing the hands back toward the chest, then pressing down to waist height.

FORM 8 GRASP THE PEACOCK'S TAIL (RIGHT SIDE)

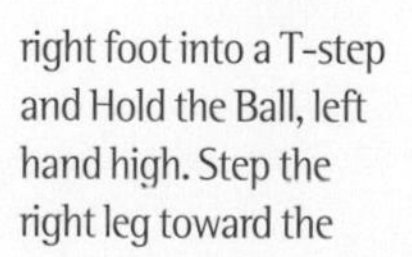

The arms should separate as the weight shifts to the left leg. To Ward Off, bring the right foot into a T-step and Hold the Ball, left hand high. Step the right leg toward the right wall and lift the right arm. At the same time, lower the left hand past the right wrist and down to the left hip. To Roll Back, turn the waist slightly to the right, at the same time

how's it going?

As you push forward in the Press movement, do not lean forward. Keep the elbows slightly bent, even in the final stages of the technique. All four moves are practiced without fully extending the arms. At the end of Squeeze, the elbows should be slightly down and comfortable.

▲how's it going?

Push your weight forward, lowering your left toes to the floor, and pushing both hands upward and forward in a double-push position. To change direction, sit back onto the right leg and turn the waist to the right while turning the left toes to the front wall.

turning both palms as shown. Draw the hands down to the waist and bring the weight to the back leg. Continue the motion of the arms to point to the front wall. Press the left and right palms together to form the Squeeze posture (left hand innermost). As before, sit back and then forward in the Double Push motion to complete the Press Position.

form 9 ▶▶

2

forms 7–12 continued

This is the first occasion where the Hook Hand is used. This unusual hand shape should not cause strain or tension in the wrist or fingers. The transitional to enter the Single Whip is repeated later to form a movement called Hands Like Clouds.

FORM 9 SINGLE WHIP

Sit back and turn your right toes to face the front wall. At the same time, arc your right hand down and across the body to rest at the left hip with the palm facing up. Raise your right hand to chest height and lower the left hand to hip height. Transfer the weight back onto the right leg, turning the waist to the front right corner while turning your left palm to face upward and your right palm to face the front.

As your left leg meets the right foot in a T-step, straighten the right arm and form a Hook Hand. The left hand lifts so that the fingers point to the right wrist. As you move the left leg to face the left wall, turn the body to face the front left corner, leaving the right hand where it is.

how's it going?

Beginners tend to pass the left hand close to the face during the arcing motion. To avoid this, the arm should be kept almost straight for the duration of the move. Correct waist turning ensures the optimum gap under both armpits at all times.

how's it going?

The left hand follows the body and continues toward the left wall. The palm gradually turns to face the left wall at the same time as the turning of the right heel.

form 10 ▸▸

2

forms 7–12 continued

Here, an earlier transitional movement becomes a form in its own right, and is the only technique where Side Stepping is employed. Hands Like Clouds is an essential movement in all Yang-style routines.

FORM 10 HANDS LIKE CLOUDS

Bring your weight back as your left hand lowers to waist height. Turn the body toward the front right corner and the left toes to face the front wall. As you open the right hand, turn the left palm to face upward at waist height. At this transitional stage, if

As you move the weight back onto the left leg, turn the waist to the left. Both hands gradually turn so that the right palm faces up in front of the waist and the left arm points to the front left corner with the palm facing the front wall. Now step the right leg in to rest

how's it going?

It is initially useful to exaggerate the waist movement, as beginners tend to use only the arms, thereby closing the gaps under each arm. Do not allow your knees to buckle when side-stepping.

how's it going?

the knees are correctly aligned with the feet, the twist in the hips should feel somewhat awkward. This is only held for a moment. Lower the right hand down until the palm faces the floor at hip height. At the same time, raise the left hand to face the chin.

about a hand width from the left foot. Both feet point toward the front wall. As you take this step, raise the right hand to face height and turn the palm to face the chin. The left hand should at the same time drop to hip height with the palm facing down.

forms 10 (continued) and 11 ▶▶

2 forms 7–12 continued

During this sequence, your feet should be a hand width apart. In the third stage, the hands change heights as before and travel to the right-hand side. The right hand will be at face height and the left at waist height with the palm facing down.

FORM 10 HANDS LIKE CLOUDS CONTINUED

Turn the body toward the right corner and shift the weight to the right leg. The arms both move toward the right while turning. At the end of the movement, the right arm will point to the

FORM 11 SINGLE WHIP

Extend the right arm and form a Hook Hand. The left hand lifts so that the fingers point to the right wrist with the palm facing the chin. As you move the left leg to face the left wall, turn the body to face the front left corner, leaving the right hand where it is.

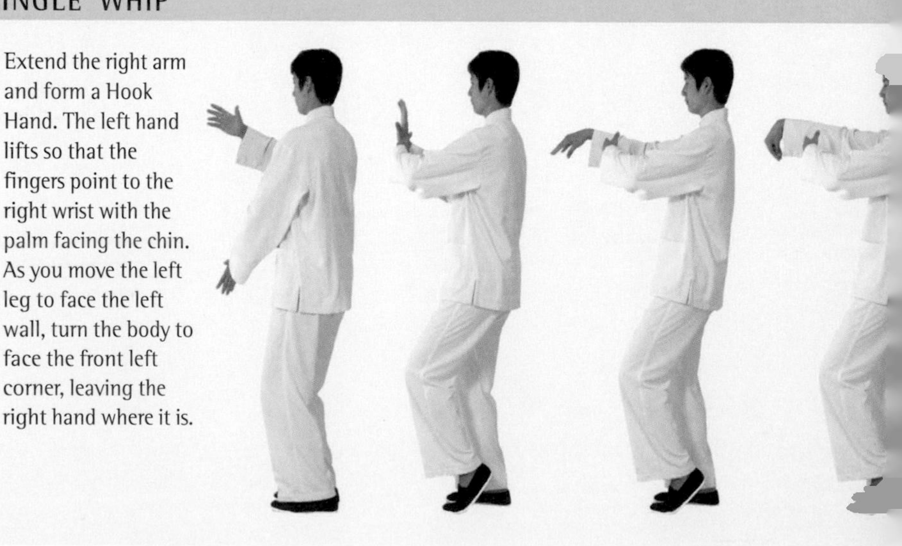

how's it going?

Often we forget to maintain a Hook Hand during Single Whip, but practice will reduce this error. The feet tend to end too narrow, but remember that, just as in Part the Wild Horse's Mane, a three-fist width is required for this technique.

how's it going?

right corner with the palm facing the front and the left hand will have the palm facing up at hip height. Take a step to the left with the left leg to leave a gap between the feet of around two shoulder widths. This leads us into the second Single Whip.

The left hand follows the body and continues toward the left wall. The palm gradually turns to face the left wall to match the movement of the right heel.

2

forms 7–12 continued

This form combines the foot movements of White Crane Spreads Wings with the hand gestures of Repulse the Monkey. The only adjustment is that in its final resting place, the left hand lies next to the right elbow, rather than at the dan tien. One martial application of this posture is to control an opponent's right elbow with your left hand, while, at the same time, striking with your right hand.

FORM 12 HIGH PAT ON HORSE

From the Single Whip position, take a Half Step forward with the back leg. During this Half Step, gently extend the left hand. As the heel lowers to touch the ground, turn the waist slightly to the right and open the right hand, keeping the left hand in the same space. At the same time, turn both palms to face upward and look toward the right hand. Your weight should now be fully supported by the right leg.

how's it going?

In the final position, be careful not to close the gap under the left arm. To avoid this, face the body just to the left of the left wall. Often the right knee will collapse and almost touch the left knee. Be sure to keep both knees in line with their respective toes. The back foot should point to the front left corner while the left foot points to the left wall.

how's it going?

Bend the right elbow so that the hand travels toward the face. Continue moving the hand forward, toward the left wrist (palm down) while at the same time lifting the left heel from the floor. As the right hand finishes its forward motion, bring the left hand with the palm facing up toward the dan tien and move the left foot a small step forward onto the ball of the foot. The left-hand fingers should point to the left elbow.

form 13 ▸▸

3 forms 13-18

This form presents an interesting challenge to strength, flexibility, and composure. The center of gravity is raised, and the entire body weight is supported on one leg. The Heel Kick should be held for two seconds at almost full extension of both legs.

FORM 13 SEPARATE AND HEEL KICK (RIGHT SIDE)

Turn the waist to the right as your left hand creeps along the right forearm until the wrists are back to back. At the same time, bring the left leg in to rest by the right in a T-step. As your left heel steps to the back left corner, turn the left palm to face the right wrist. Place the left toes down as you transfer your weight to the left leg.

Separate the arms at shoulder height until the left arm points toward the back wall and the right toward the front left corner. Position yourself so that you are looking toward the right-hand fingers. As your weight shifts to the left leg, the right leg steps in to form a T-step. Lower both arms in an arc, crossing the wrists at waist height.

how's it going?

Ensure the stability of the body before extending the kick, since this is the point where your balance is most likely to falter. The toes should be pulled back during the kick, but this may encourage the knees to lock. Do not allow this to happen, as it will adversely affect your balance.

▲how's it going?

The left wrist should be lying on top of the right. Lift the crossed wrists to shoulder height while raising the right knee to about waist height. Aim the right knee to point toward the front left corner. Separate the arms in a gentle rising and then falling arc on each side of the body, while straightening the knee to form a Heel Kick no higher than the hips.

3 forms 13-18 continued

This relatively simple form separates the two kicks and allows us to regain composure after the previous challenge and prepare for the next. The motion of the arms is symmetrical, aiding balance as the foot lowers to the ground. In the final posture, try not to raise your elbows; this means that the strike is to the underside of the ears.

FORM 14 BOX TIGER'S EARS (TRANSITIONAL TURN)

As you bend the right knee, arc both arms in front of your body toward the front right corner with your palms turned up, again maintaining your upper body symmetry throughout.

As you bend the supporting leg, lower both hands down to waist height.

Extend the right heel to the front left corner and bring your hands into your waist (as shown above).

how's it going?

In the final position, the arms are shaped as if you are about to open heavy curtains. The upper arms are parallel to the floor and the shoulders are relaxed. Do not over-reach or unbalance the body. Make sure that the elbows end up at around shoulder height. There should be no strain in the arms.

how's it going?

Gradually form a fist with both hands and arc the arms up and forward while transferring your weight forward onto your right leg. At the end of the move, the fists travel toward one another at nose height until they rest approximately two palm widths apart.

Remember to adjust your back heel so that your toes point toward the left wall.

form 15

3

forms 13-18 continued

A 180-degree turn leads us to the second of the Heel Kicks. By stretching the arms away from the body, a sense of centering and composure may be achieved. The left Heel Kick is a mirror image of the earlier kick.

FORM 15 SEPARATE AND HEEL KICK (LEFT SIDE)

Before starting the next technique, bring your weight onto the left leg, turning the right toes to face the back wall while opening and separating the hands. Look toward the left hand. As you lower the hands toward one another, bring the weight to the right leg and place the left foot by the right heel. The right wrist should rest on top of the left wrist at waist height.

how's it going?

The arms should trace a circular line during the transition, combined with the smooth nimble adjustments of the feet. Ensure the stability of the body before extending the kick. This is where inexperienced students tend to lean back, causing a loss of balance.

how's it going?

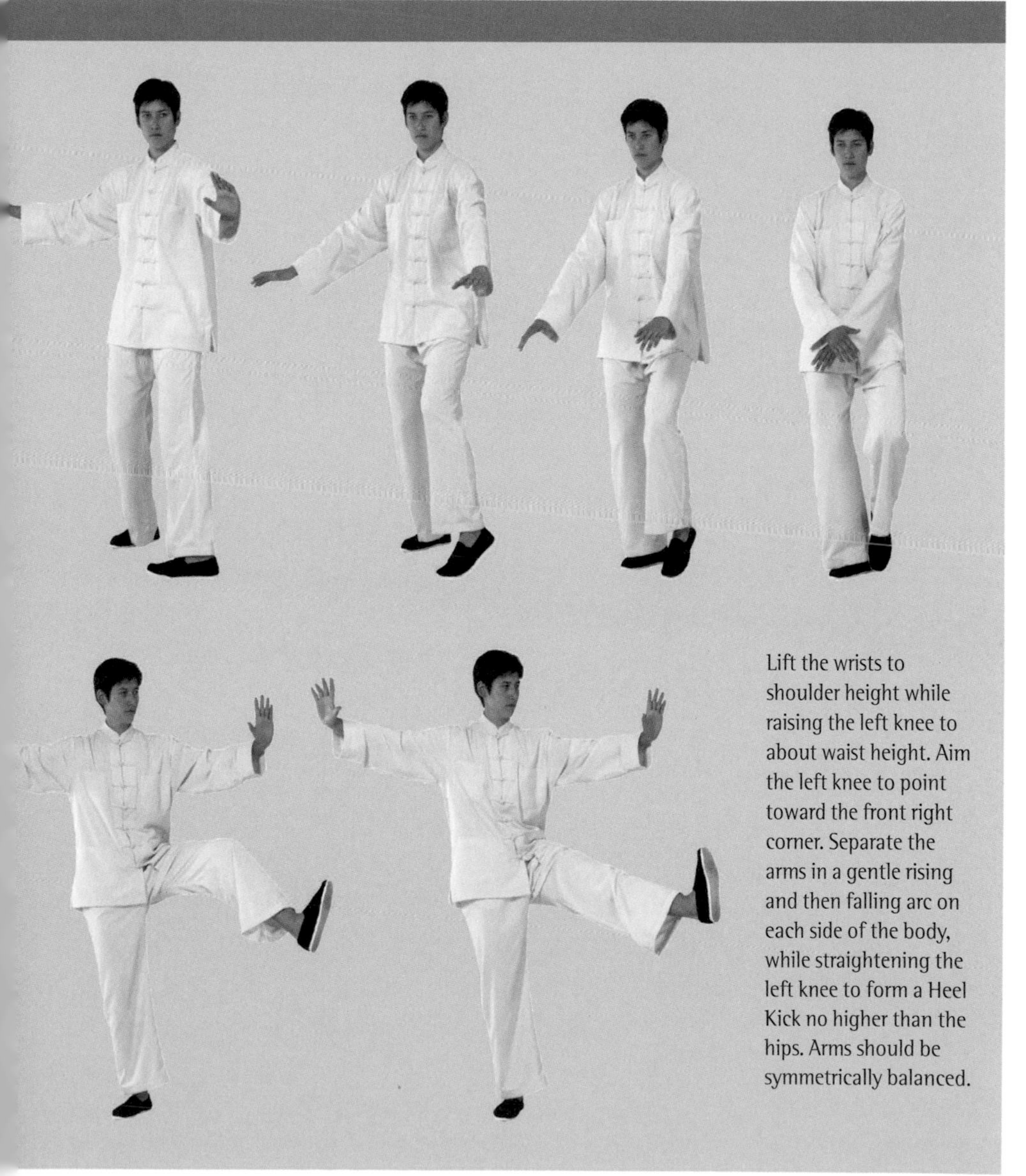

Lift the wrists to shoulder height while raising the left knee to about waist height. Aim the left knee to point toward the front right corner. Separate the arms in a gentle rising and then falling arc on each side of the body, while straightening the left knee to form a Heel Kick no higher than the hips. Arms should be symmetrically balanced.

3

forms 13-18 continued

These two techniques, which combine to form a single posture, contain the two extremes in height of the Yang style. The Snake is the lowest stance and the Rooster portion stands on an almost straight leg, bringing the body to its tallest stance.

FORM 16

SNAKE CREEPS DOWN AND GOLDEN ROOSTER STANDS ON ONE LEG (LEFT SIDE)

Bend the left knee and form a right-hand beak as the left hand gently arcs up and then down toward the right hand, left fingers pointing to the right wrist. Bend the supporting leg and step the left leg, toes first, toward the right wall. Simultaneously lower your left hand to the

Check your right knee alignment before going any further.

Now form a low left Bow Stance, turning the right toes forward while extending the left arm, as the right-hand beak lowers. Then point the left fingers up while rotating the right arm until the beak fingers

how's it going?

Although Snake Creeps Down implies a low stance, do not sacrifice good posture. The height you can achieve is governed by individual ability, flexibility, and anatomy. It is important to keep the back straight and upright throughout the exercise. The transition to the next stance should be even and fluid.

how's it going?

right hip. The weight is on the right leg, and the feet are roughly parallel.

While turning the body to face the back right corner, turn the left toes

and the left-hand fingers to point toward the right wall. The left

palm should face the back wall, aiming the fingers toward the right wall.

point upward. Turn the left toes slightly to the left and lower the

left hand to the side of the waist with the palm facing downward.

At the same time, raise the right knee and the right hand forward to

form the Golden Rooster position.

3 forms 13-18 continued

This form reflects the corresponding left-side technique. If the left side was learned thoroughly, this side should not present a great challenge to master. Through practice, both will gradually feel equally comfortable.

FORM 17 SNAKE CREEPS DOWN AND GOLDEN ROOSTER STANDS ON ONE LEG (RIGHT SIDE)

As you bend the supporting leg, step the right leg, toes first, toward the right wall as you lower the right hand. The feet should be roughly parallel and the weight should be to the left. Turn the right leg on its heel and point the right-hand fingers to the right wall while at the same time turning the body to face the back left corner.

how's it going?

As you finish a long Bow Stance (see p. 26) after Snake Creeps Down, be sure to maintain a sufficient width between your feet to provide stability for the single-leg stance. The Bow Stance should be about two fists' width. When "creeping down," ensure correct left knee alignment, as misalignment can cause painful knee discomfort.

▲how's it going?

Now, push the weight forward onto the right leg while extending the right arm forward. The left hand sinks down to waist height, still forming a beak. As you turn the left toes to face the back left corner, point the fingers of your right hand upward and rotate the left arm until the fingers of the beak point upward. Turn your right toes slightly to the right and lower the right hand to the side of the waist with the palm facing down. At the same time, raise the left knee and the left hand to complete the Golden Rooster Stands On One Leg.

3 forms 13-18 continued

As in the previous posture, this technique is performed on both the left and right sides. But unlike before, both sides will count as one movement. In this case, the final posture of each side ends facing a corner.

FORM 18 FAIR LADY WORKS THE SHUTTLES (BOTH SIDES)

Step forward with your left leg, with your toes pointing toward the front right corner. Bring the right leg in and form a Hold the Ball position with the left hand on top. Step to the back right corner with the right heel and extend the right hand to mirror the leg.

Lower the left hand to the side of the waist. As your weight transfers to your right leg, lift the right hand as if to shade you from the sun above. At the same time, lift your left hand and push the palm of that hand toward the back right corner.

how's it going?

Since this posture requires a diagonal step into Bow Stance (see p. 26), it is tempting to close the width between the feet. In the same way as a regular forward-facing Bow Stance, there should be a slight width maintained between the feet. It is also tempting to lift the shoulder of the "shading" hand and to over-extend the "pushing" arm. To avoid this, keep both arms relaxed and the back erect.

how's it going?

Sit back onto your left leg and turn your body and left hand slightly to the left. As the weight moves forward onto your right leg, bring your left leg to the right ankle and move into a Hold the Ball position with the right hand held high. Step to the front right corner with the left heel and extend the left hand to mirror the leg. Lower the right hand to the side of your waist. As your weight transfers to the left leg, lift the right hand as if to shade you from the sun. At the same time, lift the right hand and push the palm toward the front right corner.

forms 19 and 20 ▸▸

4 forms 19-24

The views shown below pan from the back wall to the front wall perspective to best show the movement. We again see the Half Step (see p. 28), although the final position may be held lower than in previous Empty Steps (see p. 26).

FORM 19 NEEDLE AT SEA BOTTOM

Take a Half Step with the right leg and extend the right-hand fingers to the front right corner. Lower your right heel, pointing your foot to the back right corner. Turn your body to the right. Bring the right hand across the waist to the right hip; lower the left across the body.

FORM 20 FAN THROUGH BACK

Return the body to an upright position and bring the left foot to meet the right. At the same time, lift the right hand to face height and raise the left hand until the fingers are almost touching the right wrist. At this point, the palm of your right hand should face the front wall and the left palm should face the left wall.

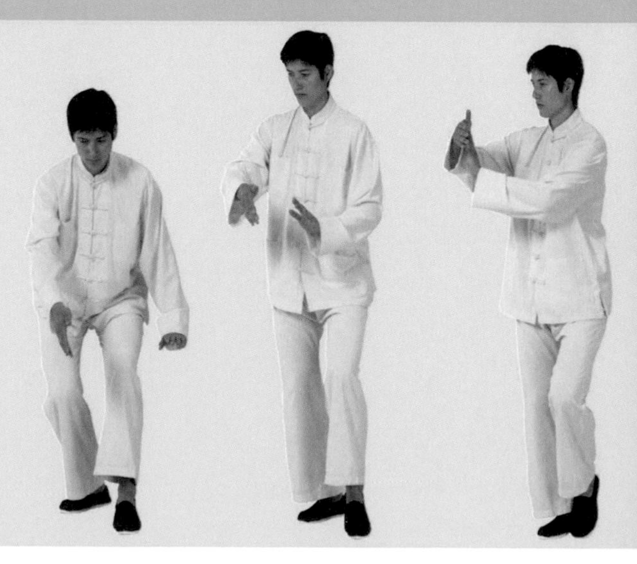

how's it going?

If the knees are touching in the final posture, this indicates poor alignment. Check that your knees point in the same direction as your toes. When inclining the body, gently pull the chin back to avoid arching the back. Check also that in Fan Through Back, both shoulders remain down, as hunching is common here.

how's it going?

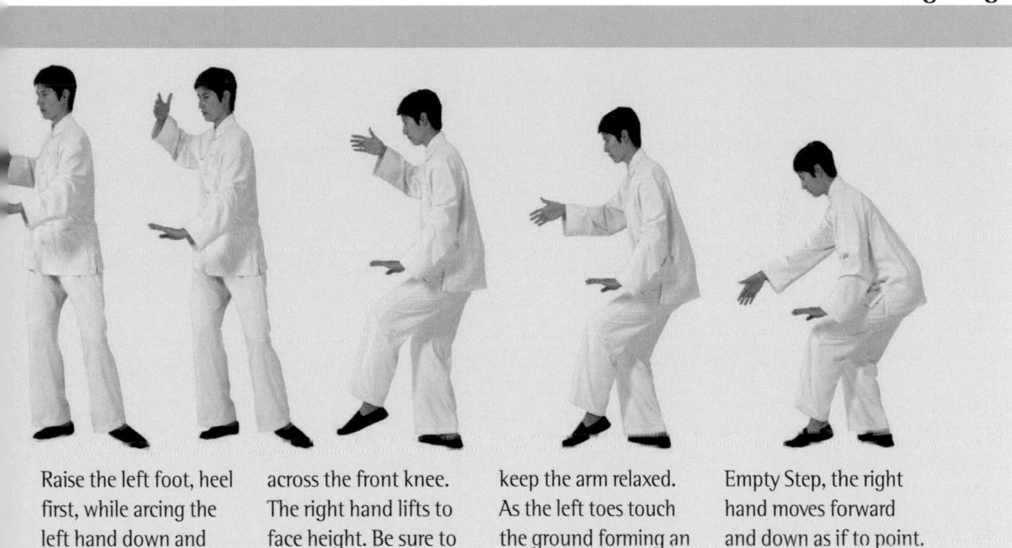

Raise the left foot, heel first, while arcing the left hand down and across the front knee. The right hand lifts to face height. Be sure to keep the arm relaxed. As the left toes touch the ground forming an Empty Step, the right hand moves forward and down as if to point.

As the left heel steps forward, start to turn the right palm toward the back wall. As your weight shifts forward to complete the Bow Stance, push the right hand toward the back wall and the left hand toward the right wall. The right hand should rest a little higher than the left one.

form 21

forms 19-24 continued

This form is made up of three parts, but it is so popular in tai chi that its components are rarely separated. The Bow Stance here is more narrow than usual (about one fist width), and is shared only with the Ward Off form.

FORM 21 DEFLECT, PARRY, AND PUNCH

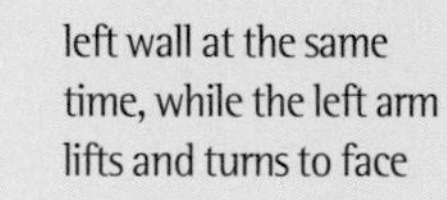

Sit back onto the right leg and turn onto the left heel until the toes point to the back left corner. The right arm should arc toward the left wall at the same time, while the left arm lifts and turns to face the back wall. As the weight returns to the left leg, the right arm

Turn the waist as you push the weight onto the right leg, pointing the toes to the front left corner. The right hand turns out while arcing to the right, still forming a fist. The left hand follows the path of the right hand until it is pointing almost to the left wall. As the left

how's it going?

All three components in this form should flow seamlessly from one to the next, while still demonstrating the characteristics of each part. Be careful not to segregate each part of the form. The narrow Bow Stance often presents a problem in balance, but this can be overcome through practice.

how's it going?

lowers to the waist forming a Fist, palm facing down. Lift and

place the right heel on the ground. The motion of the right leg mimics

the right hand as it lifts to the left of the body and forms a "back-

hand" strike aimed to the left wall. The left hand drops to the waist.

leg steps through to begin a Bow Step, the left hand turns to Parry.

Meanwhile, the right hand continues its motion to rest by the

waist with the palm facing up. As the weight shifts forward to

complete the Bow Step, the right hand travels forward to Punch.

4

forms 19-24 continued

This form is identical to the Press segment of Grasp The Peacock's Tail found in form 7, but starts from Punch instead of Squeeze. Apparent Close Up refers mainly to the crossing of the arms, whereas Press refers to the downward and forward motions.

FORM 22 APPARENT CLOSE UP

As your waist twists slightly to the left, place the left hand– with the palm facing up– under the right forearm. Sit back onto the right leg, lifting the left toes. At the same time, the right forearm passes ("threads") over the left hand. Separate the hands a shoulder width, and arc both hands backward and downward to rest the palms down at the waist. Open the right hand as it makes the threading movement. This shows the view from the front wall. Now transfer the weight forward as you lift and push your hands to face the left wall. This final posture is called "double push." Be sure not to lock the elbows at any time during this movement.

FORM 23 CROSS HANDS

Sit back and turn the left toes to face the front wall. Turn the body to the front wall, pointing each arm to its respective front corner, and turn the right toes to point to the front right corner. Circle the hands in a downward arc. As the hands draw closer to one another,

how's it going?

As you sit back, you may find that you are leaning too far backward, which creates unnecessary pressure on the lower spine. The shoulders will also tend to hunch as they travel back and down to the waist, which should also be avoided. In the final position, be careful not to lock or lift the elbows.

how's it going?

bring the weight back onto the left leg, turning the right toes to the front left corner. Cross the wrists, left wrist highest. Keep both knees bent as the right leg steps back to form a Preparation Step. Straighten the legs and lift the wrists to chest height.

forms 19-24 continued

This is the concluding sequence of the 24-step routine. The movement becomes progressively simpler, and is a physical representation of the "return to the beginning." Keep the body completely relaxed, with the crown of the head rising but the shoulders dropping down.

FORM 24 CLOSING FORM

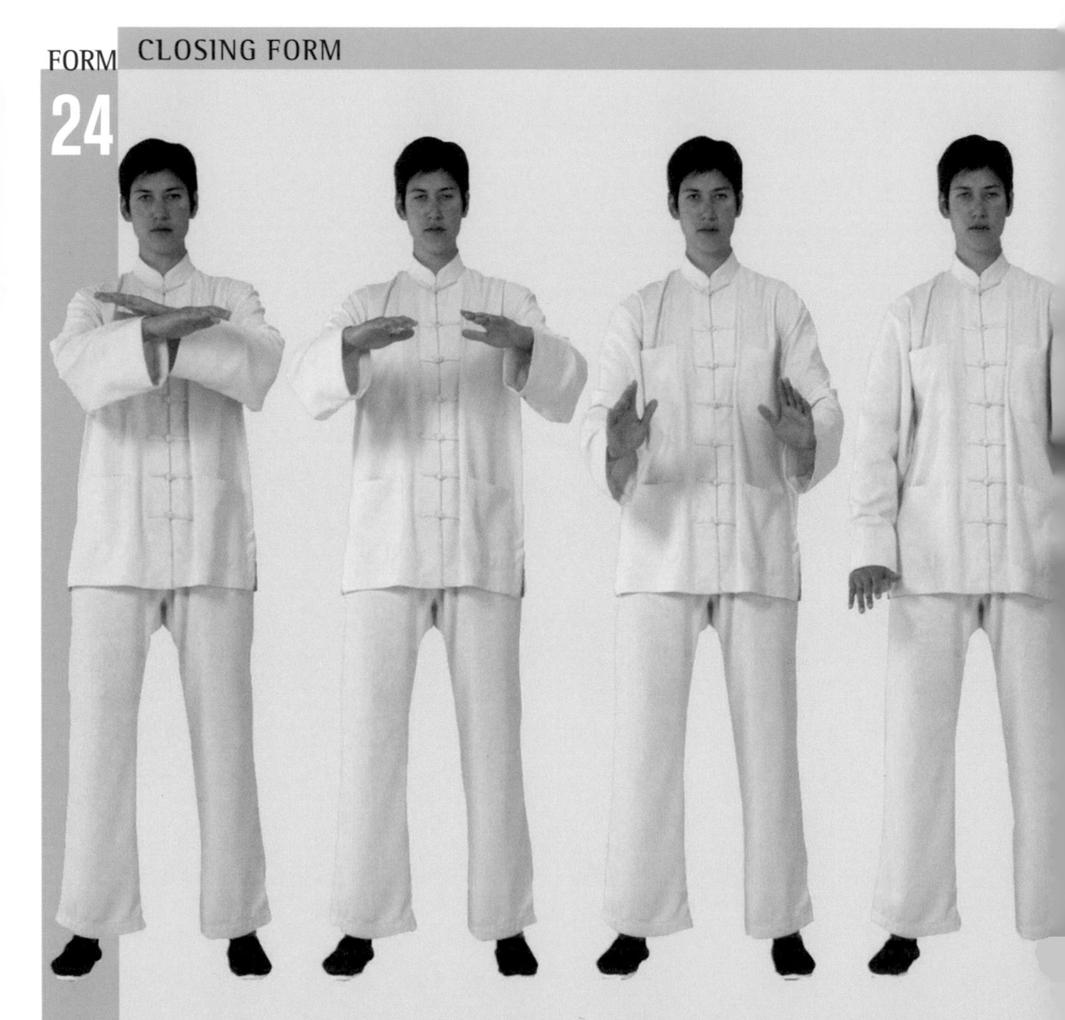

Gently lift the elbows as you stretch the arms forward. The palms should face toward the floor as they separate and remain approximately parallel and at shoulder height. Bending at the elbows first, gradually lower the arms, arcing them down in front of the body. The wrists and elbows should come to rest at the sides at the same time.

how's it going?

When lowering the arms to the side, a frequent error is to allow the elbows to reach their destination before the hands. Coordinate the arms so that the wrists and elbows arrive at the sides simultaneously.

how's it going?

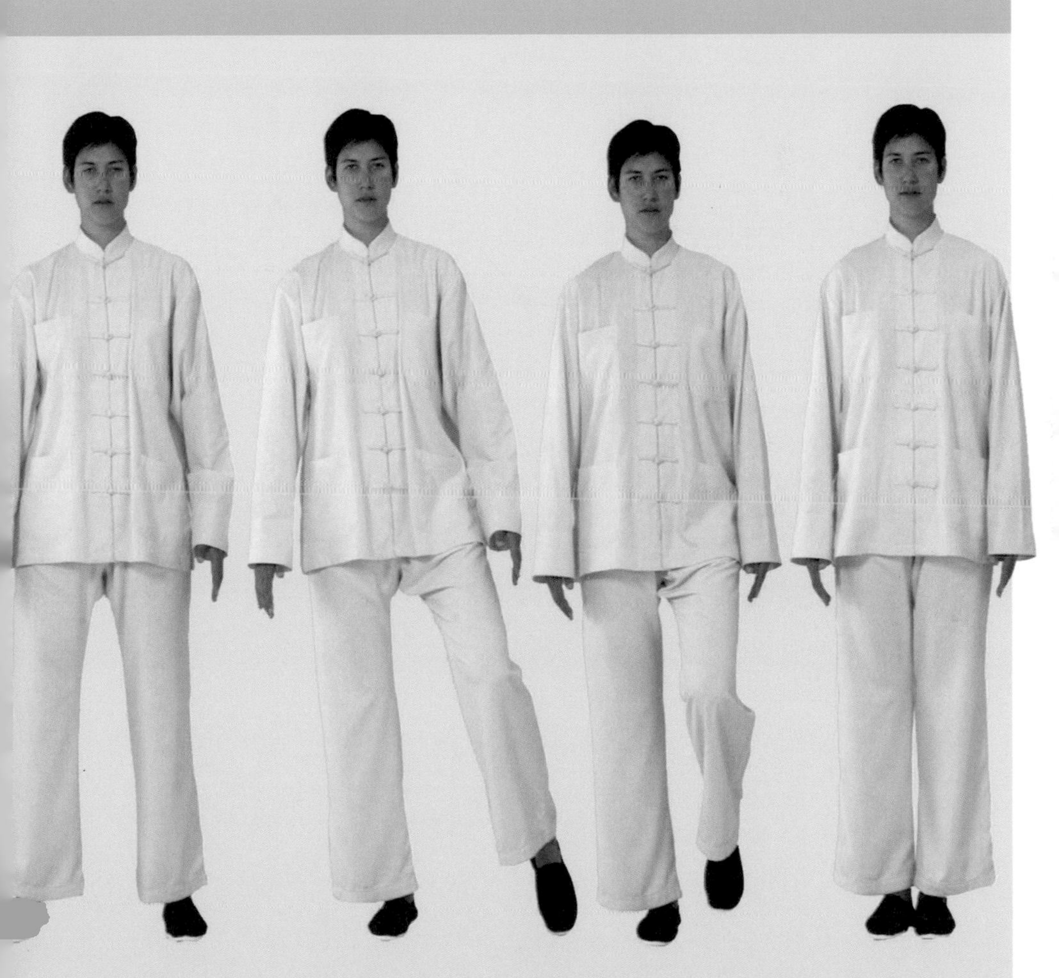

To conclude the 24-step form, raise the left-foot heel first and bring it to rest by the right leg. Place the toes down first, followed by the heel.

When you finish, your whole body should still be calm and tension free.

Stand quietly for a moment before moving.

tai chi movement guide

In Chinese martial arts, there is a saying: "There are no advanced techniques; there are only good basics." In other words, even the simplest corrections should be studied, practiced, and absorbed.

We often concentrate so much on the more challenging aspects of tai chi that we skim over the basic requirements and overlook the main pitfalls. After all, no house stands on weak foundations. The following is some basic advice relating to the pitfalls that can be encountered in each part of the body.

the back

Remain upright. Do not lean forward, backward, or to the sides. Although you may feel upright, it is always advisable to check in a mirror—you may be surprised at how wrong your position is. Our senses continually mislead us, so the feeling that we have good posture is not necessarily an accurate one.

the waist

Turning the waist is a fundamental requirement in tai chi. Correct waist movement not only improves general mobility, but also allows the upper body to relax, thereby giving you energy.

the shoulders

Perhaps the most common mistake in tai chi is to lift the shoulders rather than relaxing them. Shoulder tension is a major cause of headaches and neck stiffness, and will directly affect the muscles at the top of the spine. This causes a chain reaction of muscle compensation spreading from the backbone to the rest of the body. Avoiding this simply requires concentration and constant attention.

the arms

A general rule in the Yang style of tai chi is to maintain a gap in the armpits. This aids fluidity of movement, relaxation in the body, and encourages waist flexibility. The movements of students who do not use this gap will inevitably become awkward and robotic. Generally, the elbows are allowed to hang down from the shoulders and are not lifted unnecessarily. If they are forced upward, they will lift the

The limbs may be straight, but not locked.
The joints may be bent, but not folded.
The back should relax, but not slump.
The body should be soft, but not weak.
The legs should be strong, but not rigid.
The breath should be calm, but not shallow.
The mind should be clear, but not empty.
Such is the way of tai chi.

shoulders, thereby weakening the body.

the legs

Consisting of three main joints, we rely on our legs to support our entire body weight. Particularly when engaging in physical activity, our hips, knees and ankles are subjected to excessive forces that will often result in injury. For this reason, the alignments of the lower joints in particular should be checked regularly.

Many people have "turn outs," meaning that their toes point out at an angle when walking or standing. Over time, this slight twisting of the knees can lead to discomfort and weakened joints. Any misalignment of the knees will have an effect on the surrounding muscles and joints. If muscles develop incorrectly, they pull on the bones and joints, often causing pain. A simple but effective remedy is to point the knee in the same direction as the toes.

Although this may ache initially, eventually the area will adjust to its new alignment.

When bending the knees, do not allow them to overhang the toes. Imagine standing with the toes of one foot against a wall. Bending your knee until it makes contact with the wall is the maximum that your knee should bend in the form.

the head and neck

It is not uncommon for tai chi students to tilt their heads during tai chi practice. This mistake should be corrected from the outset. Even experienced practitioners have been known to tilt their heads in an attempt to convey the power of the sensation. This may give the impression of total absorption, but actually shows a lack of concentration. Positioning the head in a certain way can offer clues as to our inner thoughts and feelings (tilting, for example, can be a submissive or sympathetic gesture), and it is easier to project the internal state through the head than through posture. However, do not use this short cut and try to always keep the spine erect. If the head tilts, the top of the spine is bent and in poor alignment.

the hips

When standing for long periods, it is common to alleviate pressure by pushing the hips to one side and leaning the body weight on one leg. During tai chi practice, this should be avoided. Often students use this movement quite unconsciously and it is only when facing a mirror that they can see any misalignment of the hips. The nature of the stepping leads us to take short cuts during tai chi practice. For example, the Snake Creeps Down part of forms 16 and 17 (see pp. 68–71) requires the practitioner to squat low on the ground while keeping a straight back. In our effort to meet such a challenge, there is a tendency to contort the hips and lower back, causing a huge amount of physical stress on the body.

5

the learning program

Effective learning is essential to good tai chi practice. This chapter provides an effective program, demonstrating how best to develop your practice over a four-week period. It also provides a learning aid that gives the key movements in each form, designed to provide a sound basis for more advanced practice.

about learning

This program is designed to help you get the most from what you have learned. The tasks can be adapted to suit your individual lifestyle and, whether you have several hours to practice in the day or just a few minutes, you will always make progress. Try to practice at the same time each day, and thereby establish a routine.

When starting out, remember to set small achievable goals—for example, learn one posture each week instead of the whole form in a month. Be realistic. If you have only 10 minutes to spare each day, do not try to learn two movements. It is better to learn just a part of a move and be good at it than to learn the whole move poorly. Take your time. It doesn't matter if it takes several years to learn—there's no hurry. As long as you practice regularly, you will improve.

Remember that the idea of "practice" does not necessarily involve spending hours at a time on a particular move. It can be a minute here and there idly revising an arm gesture or just remembering a short sequence in your mind. There are inventive ways of working around lack of time—such as holding a stance while brushing your teeth, stretching while watching television, or reciting the form while driving.

PROGRAM A

general training guide

■ This program is simple. For each posture, repeat the motion until you feel reasonably adept at it. Once you can perform the movement without struggling, try to repeat it ten times in a row. Start with the first movement and continue through the form until you reach the end. Each day, repeat the sequence up to the stage you have learned at least three times.

■ The more times you repeat a movement, the more fluid and natural the form becomes. It is possible, however, to practice too much. If you find the first 10 repetitions are of a good standard, but the following five are poor, reduce the repetitions from 15 to 11. This will stop you from losing interest.

PROGRAM B

specific training guide

■ This is a four-week program designed for those able to practice on a daily basis, although it can be adjusted to suit individual circumstances. Before you begin any tai chi practice, go through the warm-up sequence as explained earlier (see p. 18), and take time to calm the mind through some qigong practice.

■ Do not try to do a whole day's practice in a single session and remember to take regular breaks as you practice. If you feel your training is not being fully absorbed, consider taking an additional day or two to catch up. If you are unsure about certain details, avoid rushing on to the next lesson until they are clear to you.

■ Remember that tai chi is for the individual and there is no time limit for learning the technique. An extra day, week, or month, if used constructively, will not significantly slow your progress.

WEEK 1, DAY 1

1

Learn and repeat the Preparation Step (see p. 38) six times. This step is simple and does not require much attention. Then learn the Regulate the Breath technique (see p. 39) and repeat 20 times. This can be treated as a qigong movement. Once you feel comfortable with the move, add the Preparation Step to the beginning and repeat the two parts six times.
Don't forget to take a break—if you have other things to do, then do them now. In this way, the learning task that you have just completed can be absorbed subconsciously.

2

Repeat what you learned previously without consulting the book. In the early stages you should remember just about everything. As you continue through the form, it may be harder to recall all the details, because there will be much more to remember. Now move on to the transitional posture—Hold the Ball (see p. 38). Practice from the end of Regulate the Breath to the end of the Hold the Ball position. Do this six times.

3

Next, learn the second posture, Part the Wild Horse's Mane (see p. 40), until the end of the first step. Practice this segment until it feels relatively comfortable. Then add all parts together from the beginning to the first repetition of Part the Wild Horse's Mane, and repeat this at least eight times. Consult the book to ensure that you are following the positions as accurately as possible, and practice any amendments. Do not learn any more today.

WEEK 1, DAY 2

1

Begin this session by reviewing what you learned yesterday without consulting the book. After at least four repetitions, check the book for anything you are unsure of. It is important that mistakes are corrected early on.

2

Once you have done six repetitions in a row, the sequence will embed itself in your memory. A corrected movement repeated just once or twice will not be retained as readily unless you are a proficient learner.

3

If the Hold the Ball and Part the Wild Horse's Mane positions were learned well on the left side, the right side should be relatively easy. Learn and practice the right sequence until the end of Part the Wild Horse's Mane. Practice from the beginning to this point at least six times. This Hold the Ball and Part the Wild Horse's Mane left and right sequence can be linked together to form a continual loop, alternating from one side to the other. Isolating a particular move or short sequence is a useful exercise that can be readily applied to any position that follows.

4

When you feel comfortable with the order and practice of the routine this far, go on to the third posture, White Crane Spreads Wings (see p. 42). Although it is relatively simple, it will still require a little effort. Repeat this single movement at least six times. Once this move can be performed with ease, add it to the form as learned so far and repeat eight times. If you feel confident so far, move on to the Brush Knee and Twist Step technique (see p. 44). Again, practice until your movements are fluid and performed without hesitation. Do not learn any more postures today.

about learning continued

WEEK 1, DAY 3

1 Review the previous steps. When you feel reasonably competent, move on to the next two techniques—Brush Knee and Twist Step. This should be fairly straightforward. The form requires this technique to be repeated three times, although it is beneficial to practice many repetitions in a loop as described earlier. When these three steps become familiar, move on to Strum the Lute. Practice this posture until you can repeat it six times consecutively with no obvious mistakes. When this is achieved, add it to the previous movements, and run through the form six times. Then stop—be patient and wait until tomorrow before learning any more.

WEEK 1, DAY 4

1 As before, run through the sequence you have learned up to now. If you can complete four repetitions without mistakes, go on to learn the last posture of section one, Repulse the Monkey (see p. 48). Learn all three repetitions at the same time.

2 Your movements should be thoroughly practiced until they can be performed with ease and grace. Stay on this section until you feel no hesitation. Then repeat the form from the start to the end of section one at least 20 times over the next two days before moving on. Make your movements as clear as possible.If you need to stop at any time to remember a move or part of a move, do not go on to the next section. Use the rest of the week to refine your postures and inner sensitivity. Take time to consolidate what you have learned. Moving on before you are ready will hold back your progress.

WEEK 2, DAY 1

1 Learn the first stage of Grasp the Peacock's Tail. Repeat these four movements at least six times. When you are sure you can remember it well, add the right side repetition of the technique until both sides feel equally familiar. After six repetitions, link last week's practice to what you have done today.

WEEK 2, DAY 2

1 The Single Whip technique is today's focus. The transitional link from the last move to this is worth practicing carefully. This link is an introduction to the Hands Like Clouds sequence. If you learn the linking move well, Hands Like Clouds will be less confusing. Practice today's lesson well, and don't forget to run through the whole sequence twice in a row during the day.

WEEK 2, DAY 3

1 The Single Whip–Hands Like Clouds–Single Whip sequence requires a reasonable amount of practice, but once you understand the order of each movement, it becomes much easier. Practice these three postures at least six times consecutively. When you can recall the moves easily, add them to what you have done previously, and repeat twice without any mistakes.

WEEK 2, DAY 4

1 Briefly review yesterday's lessons without referring to the book. When you can repeat the form twice without strain, move on to High Pat On Horse. The movement of the upper body resembles the Repulse the Monkey that was practiced in week one. The legs mimic the White Crane Spreads Wings posture. Spend today studying the book to ensure that nothing has been forgotten.

2 Do not learn any more this week. Run through the routine so far at least six times a day over the remainder of the week. Keep the form fresh in your mind and consolidate any parts that need particular attention.

3 A good indicator as to how well you know the routine is to practice from the middle of a move to the end. For example, try to complete the form up to this point, starting from the second Repulse the Monkey or from the middle of Hands Like Clouds. If you can do this successfully and without too much thought, you have already made great progress. You are now at the halfway juncture.

4 The third section is a little more demanding than the previous two. However, because tai chi is considered a "soft" art, it is of no increased benefit to kick high or crouch low. The emphasis is more on good posture and good balance. Practice the movements in section three with care and attention.

WEEK 3, DAY 1

1 If you feel you are ready, go on to learn the kicking sequence. This consists of Separate and Heel Kick, followed by Box Tiger's Ears, and another Separate and Heel Kick. Today's practice will demand greater balance and strength to be performed well. Devote the rest of today to these three forms. At the end of the day, attempt to combine all that you have learned and repeat at least three times.

WEEK 3, DAY 2

1 Review the complete sequence that you have been practicing without consulting the book. After at least two repetitions, check the book for any possible mistakes or uncertainties. Take an extra day or two to absorb thoroughly the lessons you feel would be of benefit.

2 If you are confident of your progress so far, continue to the next two postures—the two varieties of Snake Creeps Down and Golden Rooster Stands on One Leg. However, start by practicing one side only until you are proficient. A full understanding of the move on one side aids the learning of its mirrored counterpart.

3 If you have adequate room, this exercise can be repeated in a loop. Simply go from one end of a room to the other by linking the left side to the right side repeatedly. Although this is good practice, be careful not to twist the knees out of alignment. To avoid this, do not crouch too low. Aim to repeat both sides at least four times without hesitation.

about learning continued

WEEK 3, DAY 3

1

Fair Lady Works the Shuttles is the last of the repeated postures in the 24-step routine and is the subject of today's practice. The final position of this posture is similar to the Brush Knee and Twist Step technique. The main difference is that the hand that brushes the knee pushes upward. This knowledge is sometimes useful when attempting the final position. Work on this posture for the rest of the day.

2

Over the remainder of the week, consult the book regularly and polish any part of the form that is not proficient. Try to repeat the whole routine thus far at least six times a day. With only one section to go, you should find the new movements easier to assimilate than they were at the start of your learning.

WEEK 4, DAY 1

1

Today, work on the first two positions of section four, Needle at Sea Bottom and Fan Through Back (see p. 74). Remember to learn and practice at your own pace and not to attempt anything too adventurous initially.

2

Practice the Needle at Sea Bottom form in an almost standing position before lowering the stance, and spend some time working on the fluid transition to Fan Through Back. Repeat these two forms at least eight times.

WEEK 4, DAY 2

The transitional link to form 21, Deflect, Parry, and Punch (see p. 76), can prove to be a strain on the left ankle without due care. Be sure to practice the link at least 10 times before continuing right through to the punch. The Apparent Close Up motion is the same as the Grasp the Peacock's Tail section, so this movement should be familiar. Repeat from the beginning of the form until this point six times before moving on.

WEEK 4, DAY 3

The lesson today is relatively simple. Learn and practice to the end of the form, and repeat the new postures eight times before going through the whole routine twice.

Congratulations!

You have completed the 24-step Beijing short form. You will probably realize that there are a great deal of refinements to be made, but as long as you practice on a daily basis, you will certainly improve.

learning aids

To help remember the movements, simplify each posture into its smallest components. In the case of White Crane Spreads Wings, the move can be reduced to the following commands:

1. Take a half a step, and hold the ball.

2. Raise the right hand, place the right heel down, and turn to the right.

3. Lower the left hand past the knee, and touch the toes left forward.

It can also be further reduced to:

1. Half step, hold ball

2. Right hand, right leg

3. Left hand, left leg

Although rather simplified and lacking in detail, these small "memory hooks" often help the learning process. It may also be of use to record short commands. You can include as much or as little detail as appropriate.

glossary

advocate To endorse something.
anatomy The physical structure of the body.
ancient Of or relating to anything that is extremely old.
balance The harmonious relationship of multiple entities.
chronic Relating to anything that is long-lasting or permanent, usually a disease.
component A piece or part of a larger whole.
consideration Thought given to something.
creativity Of or relating to creating or producing, usually something artistic.
cultivate To help nurture and grow.
diaphragm The muscle that extends across the bottom of the rib cage.
ebb To flow or move backward.
efficiency The state of accomplishing the most work in the least amount of time.
encompass To fully envelope or embrace.
environment The physical and cultural surroundings of a person or thing.
flexibility The property of being easily bent.
form The method of performing a movement.
impulse The urge to do something.
limitations Restrictions on how far something can progress.
maintain To take care of or sustain.
marginal Something outside of the mainstream.
mental Having to do with the mind.
methodical The act of being cautious.
origins The place from which an entity comes.
patient A state of calm before an outcome or result.
physical Relating to the body as opposed to the mind.
position A physical configuration.
posture Correct positioning or alignment.
practitioner Someone who practices a discipline.
progression The degree of progress.
psychological Of or relating to the nature of behavior.
revitalization Reintroducing life or energy to something.
sequence The order of a series of particular events.
spiritual The state of believing in the metaphysical.
technique The method by which an act is performed.
theory A widely believed explanation of a phenomenon that is not yet proven.
torso The mid-section of the body, which excludes the head, neck, and limbs.
transfer The moving of something from one entity to another.
tuberculosis An infectious disease that affects the lungs.
venture A journey of some sort.
wellbeing The physiological state of a person.

for more information

Canadian National Martial Arts Association (CNMAA)
1359 McKenzie Avenue
Victoria, BC V8P 2M1
Canada
(250) 885-8850
Web site: http://www.cnmaa.com
The CNMAA is a nonprofit society formed in August 2005 to provide a formal structure for organizing and administering the Canadian National Martial Arts Team.

Kick Start
427 West 20th Street, Suite 203
Houston, TX 77008
(713) 868-6003
Web site: http://www.kick-start.org
Kick Start is the foundation established by Chuck Norris. Originally intended to prevent drug abuse, the organization is focused on changing and saving the lives of at-risk kids through martial arts training.

Martial Arts International Federation (MAIF)
1850 Columbia Pike, Suite #612
Arlington, VA 22204
(703) 920-1590
Web site: http://www.itkj.org/systems.html
MAIF is a forum for creating international standards for all forms of martial arts.

T'ai Chi Magazine
Wayfarer Publications
P.O. Box 39938
Los Angeles, CA 90039
(323) 665-7773
Web site: http://www.tai-chi.com
This magazine, published since 1977, features articles, interviews, tips from experts, and other resources for those interested in tai chi.

United States Martial Arts Association (MSMA)
8011 Mariposa Avenue
Citrus Heights, CA 95610
(916) 727-1486
Web site: http://www.mararts.org
MSMA is a nonprofit organization dedicated to unifying all martial arts in the United States by offering a wide range of martial arts services.

WEB SITES

Due to the changing nature of Internet links, Rosen Publishing has developed an online list of Web sites related to the subject of this book. This site is updated regularly. Please use this link to access the list:

http://www.rosenlinks.com/fctc/tai

for further reading

Boedicker, Freya, and Martin Boedicker. *The Philosophy of Tai Chi Chuan: Wisdom from Confucius, Lao Tzu, and Other Great Thinkers*. Berkeley, CA: Blue Snake, 2009.

Chuckrow, Robert. *Tai Chi Dynamics: Principles of Natural Movement, Health, & Self-Development*. Boston, MA: YMAA Publication Center, 2008.

Dougherty, Martin J. *Secrets of Martial Arts Masters*. Mankato, MN: Capstone, 2009.

Dreyer, Danny, and Katherine Dreyer. *ChiRunning: A Revolutionary Approach to Effortless, Injury-Free Running*. New York, NY: Simon & Schuster, 2009.

Gifford, Clive. *Martial Arts*. New York, NY: Marshall Cavendish Benchmark, 2010.

Gilligan, Peter A. *What Is 'tai Chi'?* London, England: Singing Dragon, 2010.

Goodman, Didi, and Linda Nikaya. *The Kids' Karate Workbook: A Take-Home Training Guide for Young Martial Artists*. Berkeley, CA: Blue Snake, 2009.

Kauz, Herman. *Tai Chi Handbook: Exercise, Meditation and Self-Defense*. New York, NY: Overlook, 2009.

Koontz, Robin Michal. *Tai Chi for Fun!* Minneapolis, MN: Compass Point, 2008.

Liao, Waysun. Chi: Discovering Your Life Energy. Boston, MA: Shambhala, 2009.

Liao, Waysun. *The Essence of T'ai Chi*. Boston, MA: Shambhala, 2007.

Muir, Gordon, and T. T. Liang. *Yang Style Traditional Long Form T'ai Chi Ch'uan, as Taught by Master T.T. Liang*. Berkeley, CA: Blue Snake, 2008.

Ollhoff, Jim. *Martial Arts Around the Globe*. Edina, MN: ABDO Pub., 2008.

Parry, Robert. *Tai Chi*. Blacklick, OH: McGraw-Hill, 2007.

Pawlett, Ray. *The Karate Handbook* (Martial Arts). New York, NY: Rosen Publishing Group, 2008.

Rones, Ramel, and David Silver. *Sunrise Tai Chi: Simplified Tai Chi for Health & Longevity*. Boston, MA: YMAA Publication Center, 2007.

Scandiffio, Laura, and Nicolas Debon. *The Martial Arts Book*. Toronto, Canada: Annick, 2003.

Stone, Justin F. *T'ai Chi Chih!: Joy Through Movement*. Albuquerque, NM: Good Karma, 1996.

War, Peter. *The Kung Fu Handbook* (Martial Arts). New York, NY: Rosen Publishing, 2008.

Yang, Jwing-Ming, and David Grantham. *Tai Chi Ball Qigong for Health and Martial Arts*. Wolfeboro, NH: YMAA Publication Center, 2010.

Yang, Jwing-Ming. *Tai Chi Chuan: Classical Yang Style: The Complete Long Form and Qigong*. Wolfeboro, NH: YMAA Publication Center, 2010.

index

ABOUT THE AUTHOR

Andrew Austin began his tai chi practice in 1990 and has been taught by many of its leading practitioners in both the U.K. and China. He has also studied at the Capital College of Physical Education in Beijing and at the Shaolin Temple. Andrew has been teaching tai chi since 1992, and has taught several British champions. He himself has won several British tai chi competitions, and has been highly ranked both in the European and world scene. In 1997, he co-founded the Zheng Dao Lo Martial Arts Academy in the U.K., where he is the Chief Technical Director. In 2002, he was presented with a national award for his contribution to Chinese martial arts by the British National Martial Arts Association.